Understanding the Maccabean Revolt

167 BCE to 63 BCE

An Introductory Atlas

Michael Avi-Yonah

Shmuel Safrai · Ze'ev Safrai

cartaJerusalem

First published in 2016 by
CARTA Jerusalem

Excerpted and adapted from
The Carta Bible Atlas
Carta, Jerusalem 2011

Carta Jerusalem, Ltd.
11 Rivka Street, P.O.B. 2500,
Jerusalem 9102401, Israel
E-mail: carta@carta.co.il
www.carta-jerusalem.com

Editor: Lorraine Kessel
Cartography: Carta, Jerusalem

Picture Sources:
Pictures are via Wikimedia Commons, are in the public domain, and have been attributed to their authors.
All other illustrations are from the archives of Carta, Jerusalem

Great care has been taken to establish sources of illustrations. If inadvertently we omitted to do so, due credit will be given in the next edition.

ISBN: 978-965-220-875-0

Printed in the United States of America

CONTENTS

THE SELEUCID EMPIRE

After the battle of Magnesia in 189 BCE, the Seleucids were forced to retreat from Asia Minor, and subjected to stringent peace conditions. Nonetheless, the Seleucid Empire remained large and powerful, encompassing all of present-day Israel and Syria, most of Iraq and almost all of Iran. The Seleucid army remained powerful and, except for Rome, none of the neighboring powers could contend with its technological superiority. Its combat technique was based on the phalanx, a battle formation consisting of sixteen or more rows of soldiers arrayed in close order, with the number of soldiers in each row dependent on the extent of the battlefield. The phalangite was armed with a long spear and shield. The densely-packed phalanx arrayed for battle with spears bristling in all directions must have been an awesome sight for less well-equipped opponents. The phalanx was flanked by light and heavy cavalry and units of "challengers" carrying pikes, and by archers and spear throwers. The aim of these auxiliary forces was to exhaust the opposing forces and inflict as many casualties as possible.

Sometimes the Seleucids used elephants to demoralize the enemy and as firing platforms, but they were mainly used for defensive purposes. Tactics were rigid and never changed. The majority of the men were recruited from the settlers of the colonies set up by the Seleucid kings. The young men served in the regular forces and their fathers made up the reserve force that was called to arms in times of emergency.

The Seleucid troops also included mercenaries, and young boys were also conscripted from among the subjugated peoples. Altogether, the Seleucid armed forces numbered between 60,000 and 100,000 combatants.

To control and rule its far-flung empire, the Seleucid army had to be highly mobile. Thus its commanders depended on quick and decisive victories. These then were the realities facing the Maccabees and influencing their strategy.

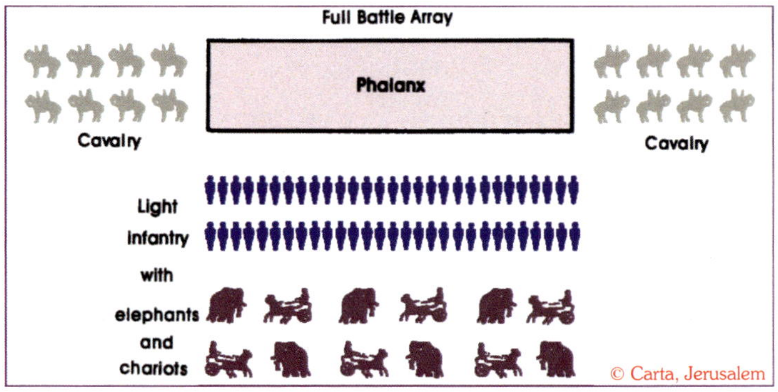

Deployment of Hellenistic Armies

Seleucid war elephant.
Carta, Jerusalem

> And they distributed the beasts among the phalanxes; with each elephant they stationed a thousand men armed with coats of mail, and with brass helmets on their heads; and five hundred picked horsemen were assigned to each beast.
> (1 Maccabees 6:35)

THE BEGINNINGS OF THE MACCABEAN REVOLT 167 BCE

Antiochus and his advisors, heeding the more extreme of the Hellenized Jews, believed that the majority of the Jewish nation was ready to accept Greek culture. Being impatient with the slow progress of Hellenization, Antiochus decided to turn the House of God into a Greek temple of Zeus or Dionysius, whom he equated with the God of Israel. The strong resistance of the people led to the first known instance of religious persecution in history: worship of God was forbidden and the Jews were forced to sacrifice to other gods. The Hellenists built a fortress, the "Acra," to secure their position in Jerusalem, and next to it a new city, in the Greek style.

The persecution led to a revolt that broke out not in Jerusalem, but in the Jewish townlet of Modiin, in the district of Lydda. Some of the leaders came from neighboring villages, such as Yose ben Joezer of Zeredah, leader of the Hasidim, pious Jews who rallied to the defense of the Law. Mattathias, priest of the Hasmonean family, and his sons refused to obey the royal order to sacrifice to Zeus. Mattathias killed a Jew who was about to obey the order, as well as the king's representative, and destroyed the altar there. Modiin itself was close to Lydda, the district capital, and thus exposed to reprisals. Mattathias and his sons fled, probably to the mountains "around Samaria" (Gophna). There they were joined by the Hasidim. From their refuge Mattathias and his men went forth, overturned the altars of the foreign gods, and roused the Jewish villages against the Hellenizers living in Jerusalem under the protection of the Seleucid army. Apollonius, commander of the troops at Samaria and governor of the region near Gophna, went out to crush the rebellion. Judas Maccabeus, who had assumed command on the death of his father Mattathias, attacked the royal troops, probably at the ascent of Lebonah, and destroyed them. Apollonius was killed in the fighting and Judas took his sword "and fought with it thereafter" (1 Macc. 3:12). In response, the Seleucid authorities removed the regions of Lydda and Gophna from Judea and annexed them to Samaria.

Mattathias
"Promptuarii Iconum Insigniorum "
Author: Guillaume Rouille, 1553
(Via Wikimedia Commons)

In those days arose Mattathias in Modiin ... the king's commissioner, who compelled men to sacrifice, he killed ... so he and his sons fled into the mountains ...

(1 Maccabees 2:1, 25, 28)

Judas Maccabeus, 10th cent., Northern Italy.
Source: Josephus
Author: Jossiponos
(Via Wikimedia Commons)

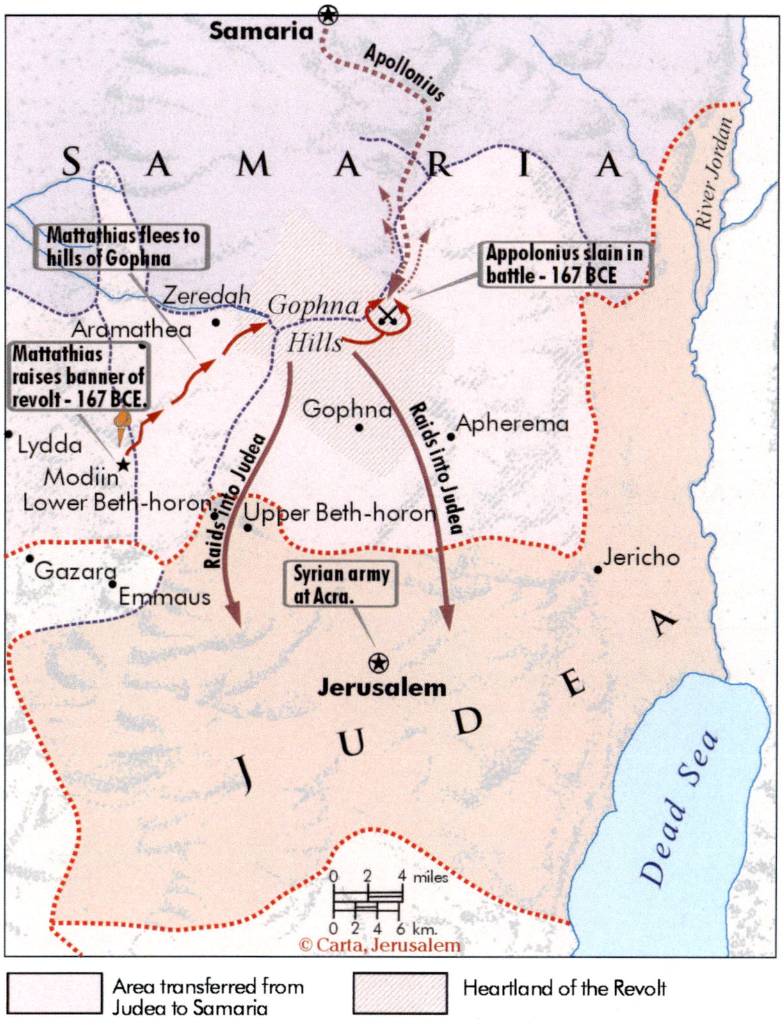

1 MACC. 2:1-3:13; 2 MACC. 8:1-7

THE BATTLE OF BETH-HORON 166 BCE

But we fight for our lives and our laws.
(1 Maccabees 3:21)

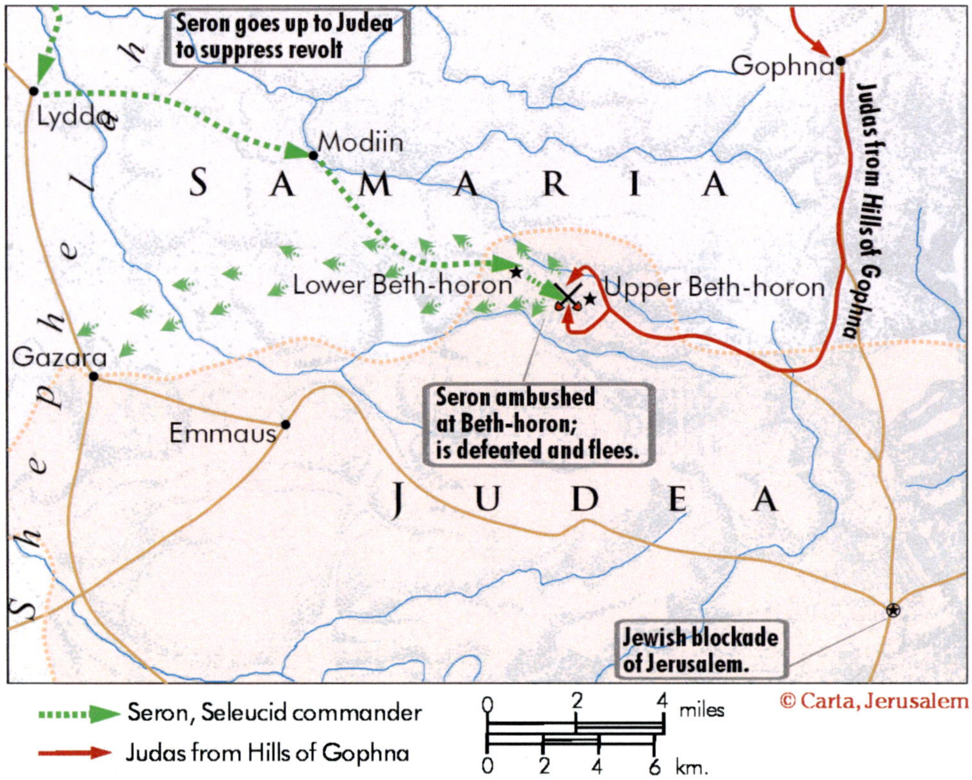

1 MACC. 3:13-24

Statue of Antiochus IV of Syria
Altes Museum: Photographer: Jniemenmaa
(Via Wikimedia Commons)

News of Apollonius' crushing defeat, and the increasing distress of the Hellenizers isolated in Jerusalem, moved Seron, a Seleucid commander, to suppress the growing rebellion. To relieve Jerusalem he chose the traditional route from Lydda by way of the ascent of Beth-horon. While Seron's men labored up the steep ascent, Judas Maccabeus unexpectedly attacked, and Seron and his men were swept before him. The remnants of the defeated army fled back to the coastal plain and retreated to "Philistia." The second attempt to break the blockade of Jerusalem had also ended in failure.

Lower Beth-horon in 1880
Source: Picturesque Palestine, Sinai and Egypt D. Appleton New York 1883
Author: Lane-Poole, Stanley. (Via Wikimedia Commons)

THE BATTLE OF EMMAUS 165 BCE

... the watchword "God's help"
(2 Maccabees 8:23)

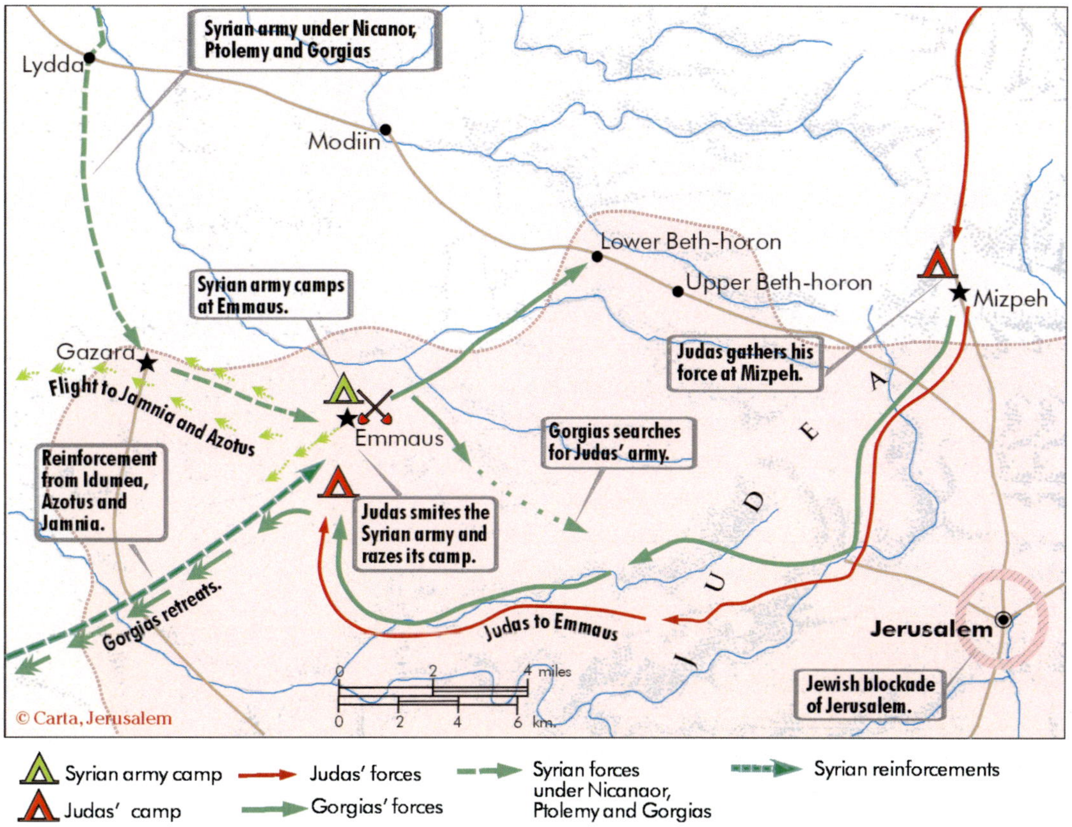

1 MACC. 3:38-4:25; 2 MACC. 8:8-29

Antiochus IV, at this time warring against Persia and Media, had entrusted the administration of the empire west of the Euphrates to Lysias, the superior of Seron. Upon Seron's defeat Lysias raised a strong army and put it under the command of Ptolemy son of Dorimenes, Nicanor, and Gorgias. The army camped at Emmaus, as the commanders feared entanglement in the mountain passes leading to Jerusalem. They were reinforced by troops from Idumea and the district of Jamnia and Azotus ("Philistia").

Judas Maccabeus rallied his men at the ancient holy site of Mizpeh. Here he was strategically placed in relation to both Jerusalem and the coast. In the end the Seleucid generals decided to seek out the rebels; Gorgias with five thousand soldiers and one thousand horsemen went out under cover of night and, guided by men from the Acra, proceeded toward the rebel camp in order to capture Judas in a surprise attack. On hearing of the division of the enemy forces, Judas Maccabeus left Mizpeh and bivouacked probably south of Emmaus. At dawn, Judas and his men (three thousand in all) advanced toward the Syrian camp. The Seleucid army formed for battle but was defeated and pursued to Gazara, the strong royal fortress at the approaches to Jerusalem. Judas restrained his men from an ill-considered chase, and while the enemy was still fleeing in the direction of Jamnia and Azotus, he returned to Emmaus to face Gorgias.

At the end of his night march, Gorgias found Judas' camp abandoned; he had worn out his men in vain. Returning to Emmaus, he saw from a hilltop that his camp was aflame. He retreated to the coast without having made contact with the rebels, and thus failed in the third attempt to free the Hellenizers encircled in Jerusalem.

Forces under Nicanor and Gorgias encamped at Emniaus; 1893 representation.
Publisher: Philadelphia, Pa., Peerless Publishing Co.
Authors: Bird, Frederic Mayer, 1838-1908 Harrison, Benjamin, 1833-1901
(Via Wikimedia Commons)

THE BATTLE OF BETH-ZUR & THE REDEDICATION OF THE TEMPLE 165 BCE

Lysias made one last attempt against the Jews. He chose the route along the watershed in Idumea, rather than endangering his forces in the narrow passes and on the steep ascents, which thrice had been the undoing of the Seleucid army. The new campaign passed along the coast to Marisa, inhabited at the time by Hellenized Sidonians and Idumeans — enemies of the Jews. From Marisa they marched with ease and arrived opposite Beth-zur, the border fortress of Judea.

The Maccabean, who surely used his interior lines of communication to follow the movements of the enemy, went forth from Beth-zur to face the invader and succeeded in repulsing the attack. Lysias retreated and Judas and his men, rejoicing, went up to Jerusalem. The fortress of Acra was still in the hands of their enemies, but the Temple Mount was regained by the Jews. Judas and his men now cleansed the Temple and repaired it after the long period of neglect. The service of God was restored after having been interrupted for three and one-half years, and they lit the lamps of the menorah to light up the Temple.

Thus, the feast of Hanukkah was observed for the first time on the twenty-fifth of Kislev, 165 BCE. Judas fortified Mount Zion (the "Mount of the Temple") and Beth-zur, "that the people might have a fortress against Idumea."

Hellenistic tomb painting at Marisa.
Carta, Jerusalem

Behold our enemies are crushed; let us go up to cleanse the sanctuary and dedicate it.

(1 Maccabees 4:36)

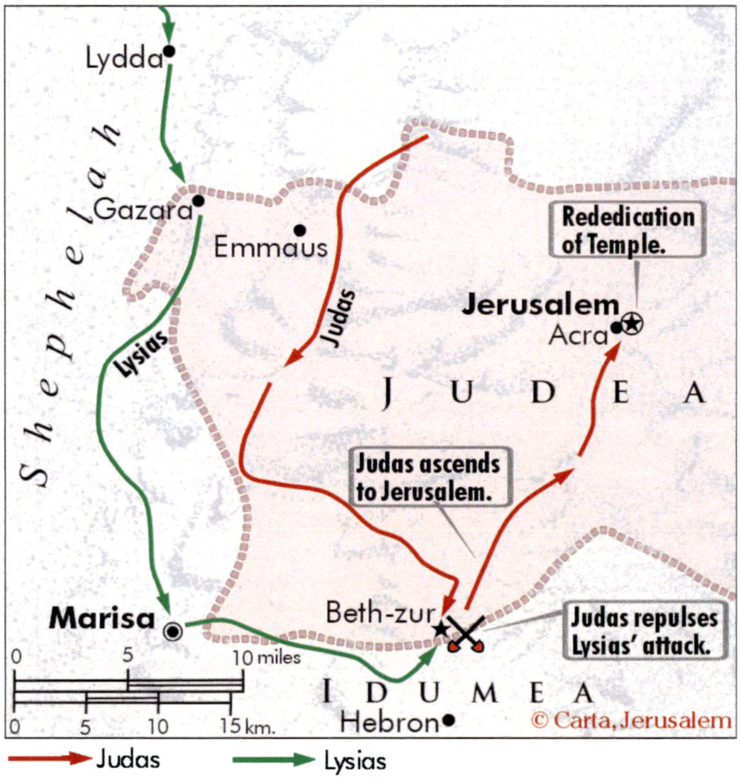

1 MACC. 4:28-61

The Ruins of Beth-zur, 1925
From: "Palaestina und das Ostojordanland"
Author: Julius Hoffmann, Stuttgart, 1925
(Via Wikimedia Commons)

JUDAS MACCABEUS' EARLY CAMPAIGNS 163 BCE

Remains of the Nabatean city of Bostra.
Author: User:Cyb3r
(Via Wikimedia Commons)

They [the heathen] determined to destroy the descendants of Jacob who lived among them.
(1 Maccabees 5:2)

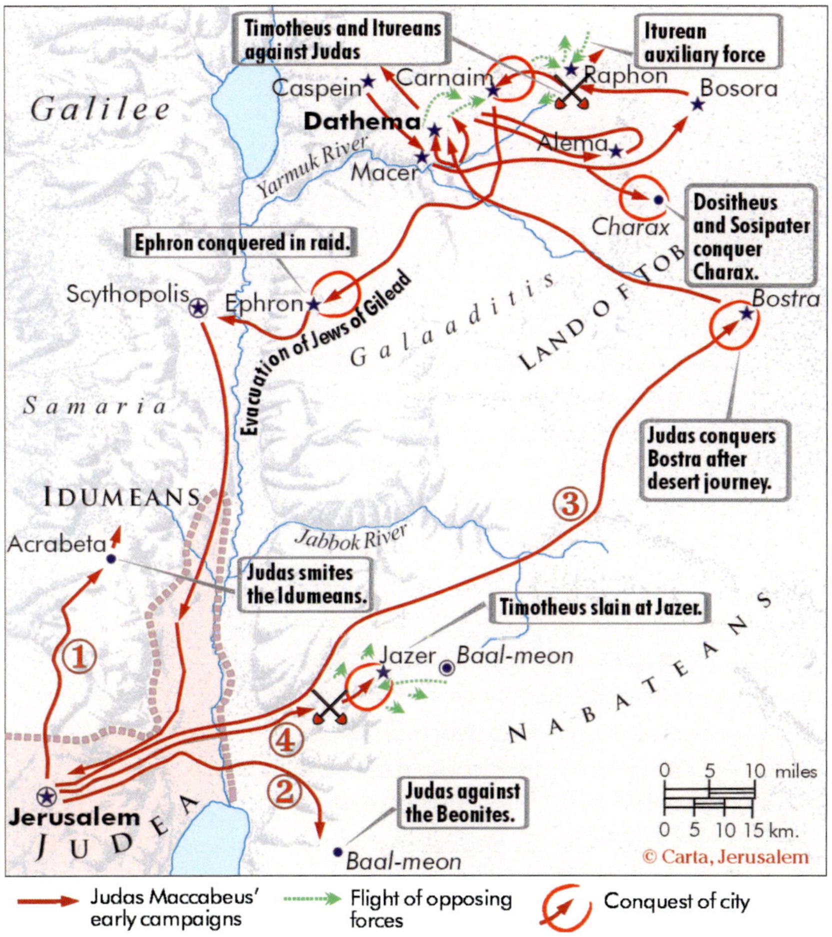

1 MACC. 5:3-13, 24-55; 2 MACC. 10:24-37; 12:10-11

Judas' successes aroused the ire of the neighboring peoples and he undertook several defensive campaigns. He first attacked the Idumeans in Acrabeta who were oppressing the Jews living among them; he mounted a similar operation against the tribe of the Beonites beyond the Jordan.

His most difficult military feat, however, was the relief of the Jewish population of Gilead. Disturbing news from there told about the persecution of the Jews, in Bostra, Bosora, Alema, Caspein, Macer, and Carnaim, all fortified cities, and in the Land of Tob. Many of the Jews fled to the fortress of Dathema and were besieged there. Judas, with his brother Jonathan and eight thousand men, set out to relieve them. Instead of going straight to Gilead, they utilized their good relations with the Nabateans east of Gilead, cut across the desert in a three-day march, and appeared, quite unexpectedly, at the gates of Bostra.

After capturing Bostra, Judas and his men marched all night, arriving at Dathema in the morning, at the very moment the enemy was about to storm the city. Judas launched a three-pronged attack on the army of Timotheus, commander of Gilead; the enemy fled on recognizing their attacker. Judas continued on to Alema, Caspein, Macer, and Bosora, everywhere relieving the beleaguered Jewish populations. Soon thereafter, Dositheus and Sosipater, commanders under Judas, overcame Charax in the Land of Tob.

Timotheus had meanwhile reorganized his army and reinforced it with auxiliary Arab troops (probably Itureans, for the Nabateans sympathized with the Jews); he confronted Judas near Raphon. In this battle too the enemy was vanquished. Judas took Carnaim and burned down the temple of Atargatis. From Carnaim Judas and the Jewish evacuees began their long march, passing through Ephron (which refused them entrance, but was taken by storm) and Scythopolis (Beth-shean), whose inhabitants received Judas cordially. The caravan finally ascended Zion with song and dance. There was one more confrontation with Timotheus, at Jazer; here too the Jews were victorious. Timotheus fell on the battlefield, and Jazer was captured.

View of Nabataen Arch at Bostra.
Photograph: Erik Hermans
Author: Institute for the Study of the Ancient World
(Via Wikimedia Commons)

SIMON'S EXPEDITION TO WESTERN GALILEE

1 MACC. 5:14-15, 20-23

So Simon went to Galilee and fought many battles against the Gentiles, and the Gentiles were crushed before him.
(1 Maccabees 5:21)

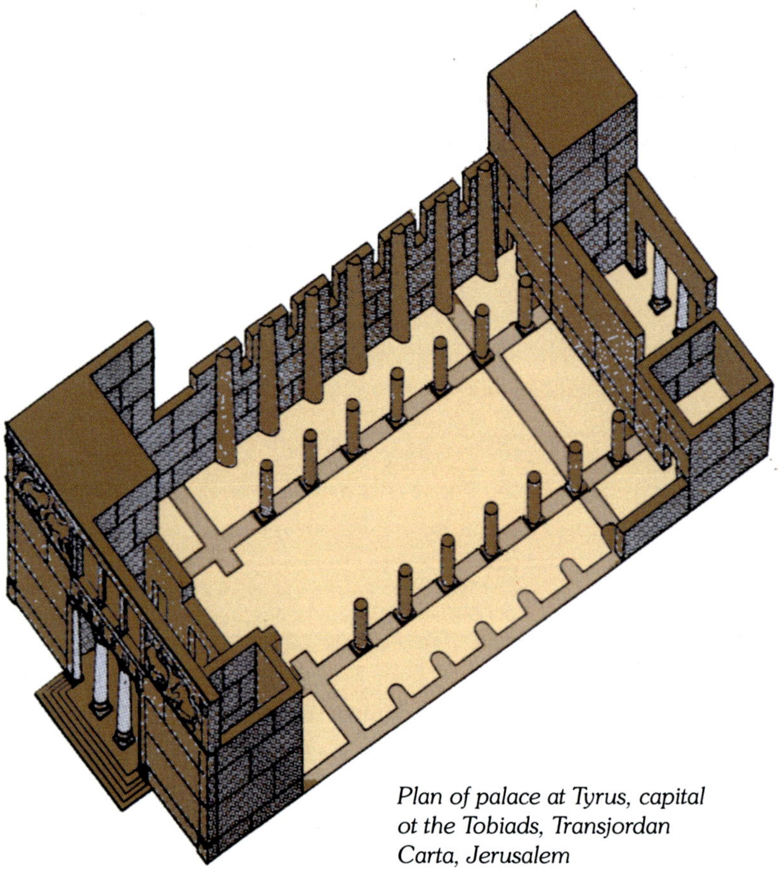

Plan of palace at Tyrus, capital of the Tobiads, Transjordan Carta, Jerusalem

While Judas campaigned in Gilead, his brother Simon at the head of three thousand men proceeded to Galilee, where the Jews had been attacked from Ptolemais, Tyre, and Sidon. Simon scattered the enemy and pursued them from Nimrin to the gates of Ptolemais. He took with him the Jews of Galilee and Arbata (several suggestions have been put forward for the identification of this city) and brought them safely to Jerusalem. It must be noted that even after this campaign Jews remained settled in the Esdraelon Valley and in Galilee.

Remains of a Tobiad palace, at Iraq al-Emir.
Photograph: Michael Gunther
(Via Wikimedia Commons)

JUDAS IN THE COASTAL PLAIN & IDUMEA 163 BCE

Afterward went Judas forth with his brethren, and fought against the children of Esau.
(1 Maccabees 5:65)

While Judas and Simon were occupied in Gilead and Galilee, Joseph (the son of Zacharias) and Azarias, two commanders who had remained in Judea, tried their luck against Jamnia. Here camped Gorgias (of the battle of Emmaus), who had probably remained behind as governor of Idumea. This action failed utterly. After Judas' return from Gilead, he himself went against Idumea. He attacked Hebron and Marisa, and even reached the gates of Azotus, and there destroyed a pagan temple.

In another campaign Judas avenged the Jews of Joppa, after their fellow townsmen had drowned them, in an act of atrocious deceit. He destroyed the port of Joppa and burned the ships. He repeated this deed at the port of Jamnia upon learning that the inhabitants of the city intended to imitate Joppa. In yet another campaign near Marisa, Gorgias was almost taken prisoner, but in the end Judas disengaged his forces and retired to Odollam in the Judean Shephelah.

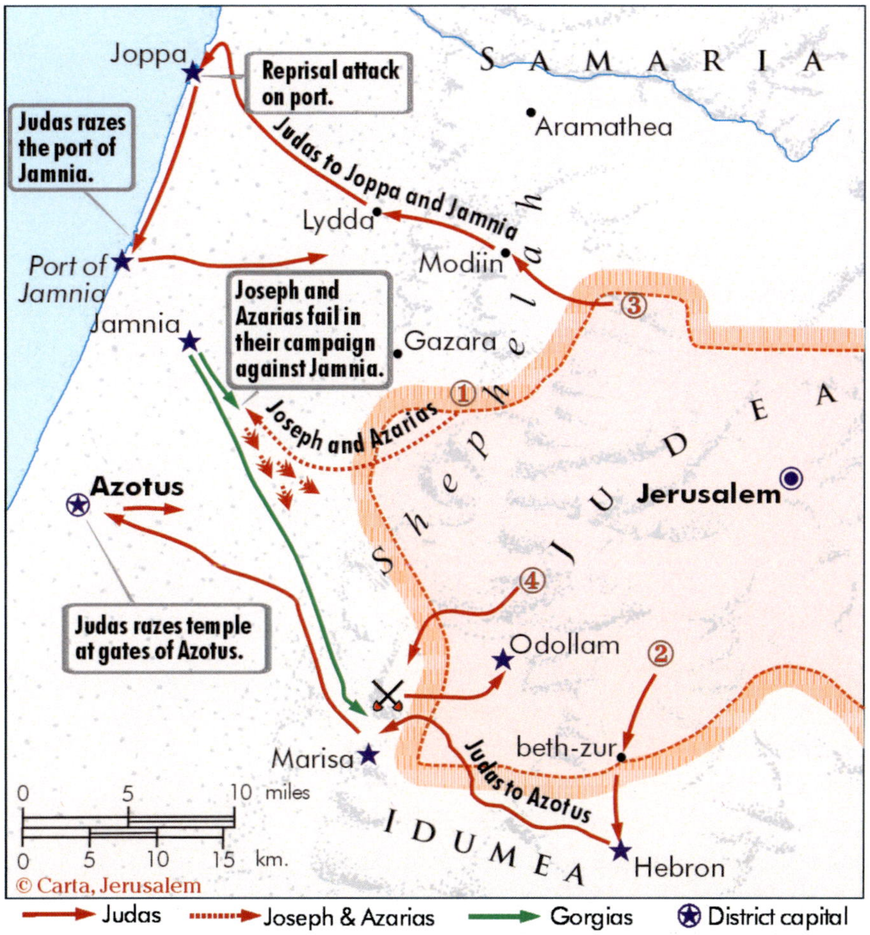

1 MACC. 5:1-2, 37-60, 65-68;
2 MACC. 12:1-15, 32-38;
ANT. 12:353

The port of the old city of Jaffa
Source: Old Jaffa
Author: Jorge Láscar from Australia
(Via Wikimedia Commons)

THE BATTLE OF BETH-ZECHARIAH
162 BCE

Seeing the strength of the king, and the violence of his forces, (they) turned away from them.
(1 Maccabees 6:47)

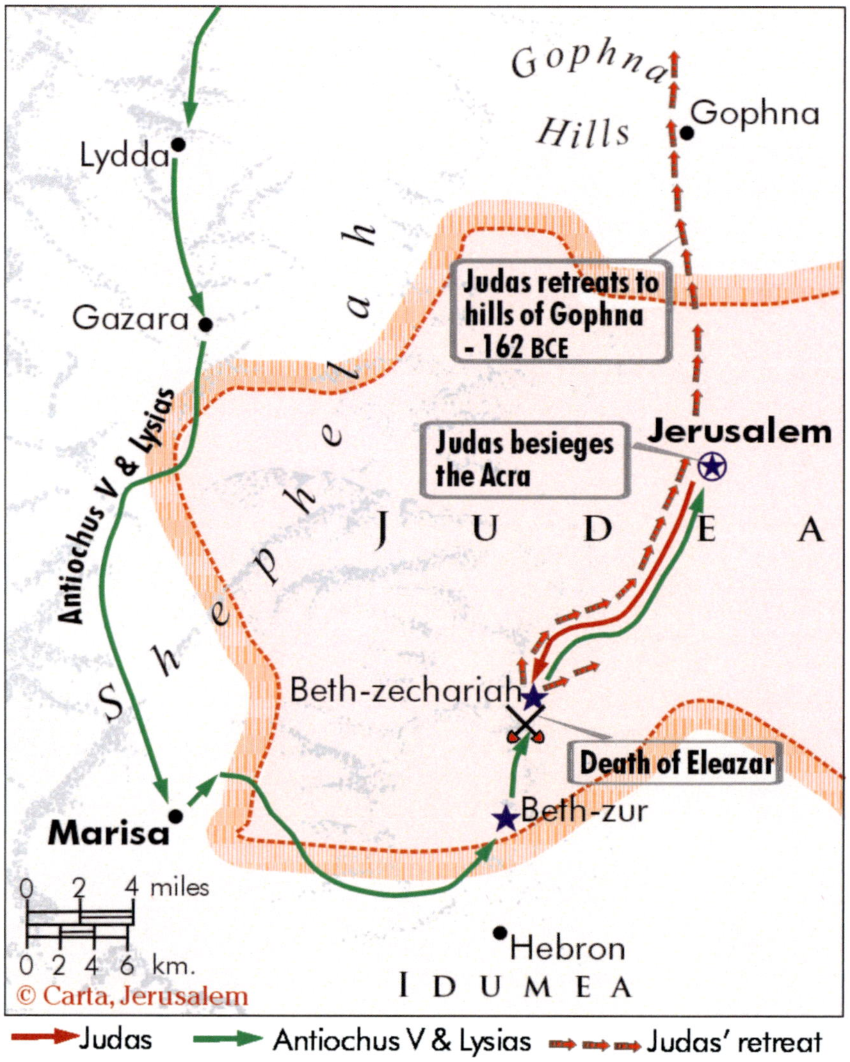

1 MACC. 6:28-63; 2 MACC. 13:1-23

Notwithstanding all the victories of Judas in remote places, Jerusalem remained divided between Mount Zion (the Temple Mount), which was in the hands of the rebels, and the Acra, which was held by the Hellenizers. On his return from campaigning, Judas beleaguered the Acra, whose inhabitants appealed to the young king Antiochus V (Antiochus IV had died in Persia in 163 BCE). In response to their call, Lysias arrived from Syria with a vast army. Having learned from experience, the Syrians took the longer but easier route through Idumea and attacked Beth-zur. Judas left Jerusalem and encamped at Beth-zechariah, north of Beth-zur. The royal army advanced toward Judas and a great battle ensued.

Eleazar (also called Avaran), the youngest of Judas' brothers, fell in this battle; in the belief that a war elephant, richly caparisoned with the king's arms, carried the king in person, he slew the animal but was thus crushed to death — the first to die of the five sons of Mattathias.

This act of valor had no influence on the outcome of the battle. The Jews "turned away from them" (1 Macc. 6:47). Beth-zur surrendered for lack of food (it was a Sabbatical year, when fields were left fallow). Antiochus and Lysias arrived at the Temple Mount and breached its fortifications. However, remembering the fierce Jewish reaction in the days of Antiochus IV, they did not interfere with the religion as such or with the Temple services. The Hasidim abandoned the revolt and Judas was forced to retreat to his original refuge in the mountains of Gophna.

Fragment of a stone door from a burial cave; Late 2nd–early 3rd centuries CE. From: The New Encyclopedia of Archaeological Excavations in the Holy Land.

THE BATTLE OF CAPHARSALAMA
162 BCE

When Alcimus saw that Judas and those with him had grown strong, and realized that he could not withstand them ...
(1 Maccabees 7:25)

In 162 BCE Demetrius I, the son of Seleucus IV, landed at Tripolis on the Syrian coast, thus starting a chain of fraternal wars within the House of Seleucus, ending in the destruction of their rule. Antiochus V was taken prisoner and put to death. The new king sent to Judea his general, Bacchides (who was in charge of the countries west of the Euphrates), with one Alcimus (Eliakim), whom he made high priest. The pious majority ("Hasidim") acknowledged in Alcimus a descendant of the high priest Aaron; they believed his promises of peace and abandoned the Maccabees, who alone persisted in their struggle for freedom.

In Jerusalem, Bacchides enthroned Alcimus, who began by slaying several leaders of the Hasidim. Bacchides, too, on his way back to Antioch, killed many of them at Beth-zetha (Berzetha).

Judas Maccabeus continued the struggle with reduced forces, and Alcimus once more had to ask for help. King Demetrius I sent Nicanor, one of the commanders in the battle of Emmaus. In one of his first actions, Nicanor tried to open the Beth-horon road connecting Jerusalem with the Seleucid bases in the coastal plain. This attempt failed at Capharsalama (near Gibeon), and Nicanor, shamefaced, returned to Jerusalem.

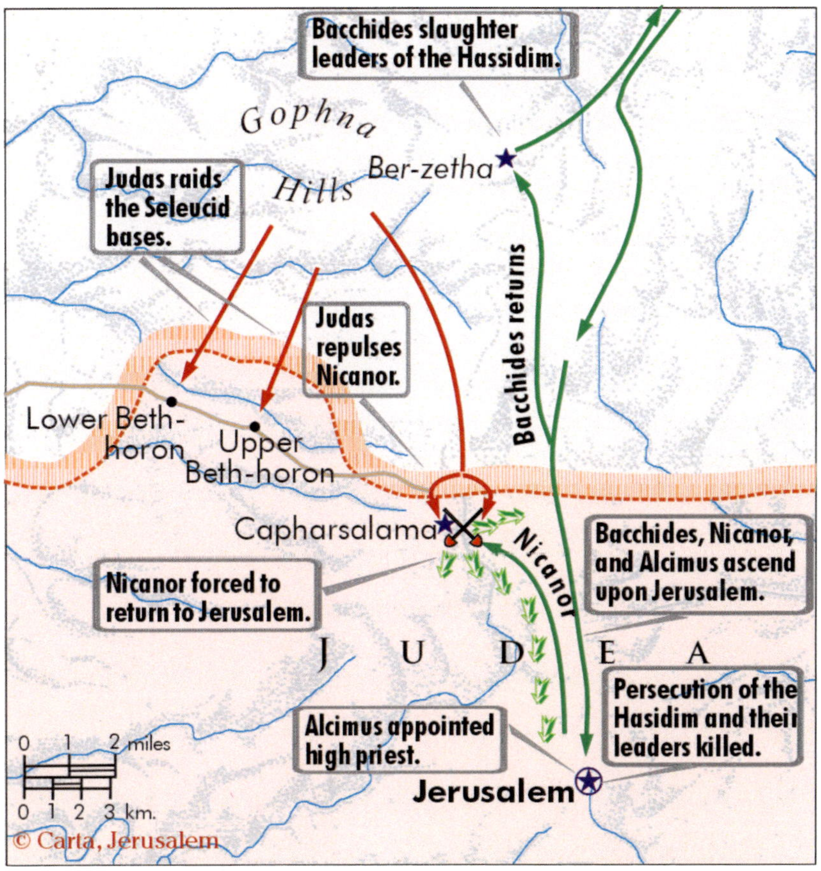

1 MACC. 7:19-31; 2 MACC. 14:15-18

Landscape of the Judean Hills; before 1906
Source: Brockhaus and Efron Jewish Encyclopedia
Author: Unknown
(Via Wikimedia Commons)

Marble bust of Demetrius I of Macedon
(National Museum in Naples
Author Saddhiyama
(Via Wikimedia Commons)

THE BATTLE OF ADASA

161 BCE

On the thirteenth [day] of Adar, the day of Nicanor.
(Scroll of Fasting)

Infuriated, Nicanor at once renewed the struggle. This time he succeeded in reaching Beth-horon, where he was joined by Syrian auxiliaries from the coast. On his way back, however, he was attacked near Adasa, south of the main highway; Nicanor, apparently, was expecting an attack from the north.

On the thirteenth of Adar (the "Day of Nicanor" of Jewish tradition) the enemy was vanquished. Nicanor himself fell in battle; his army, cut off from Jerusalem, fled in the direction of the royal fortress at Gazara, being pursued to its very gates by Judas, and by the villagers who were stirred into action by the sounding of trumpets. The day of battle was declared a holiday and was celebrated by future generations.

1 MACC. 7:39-49; 2 MACC. 15:25-28

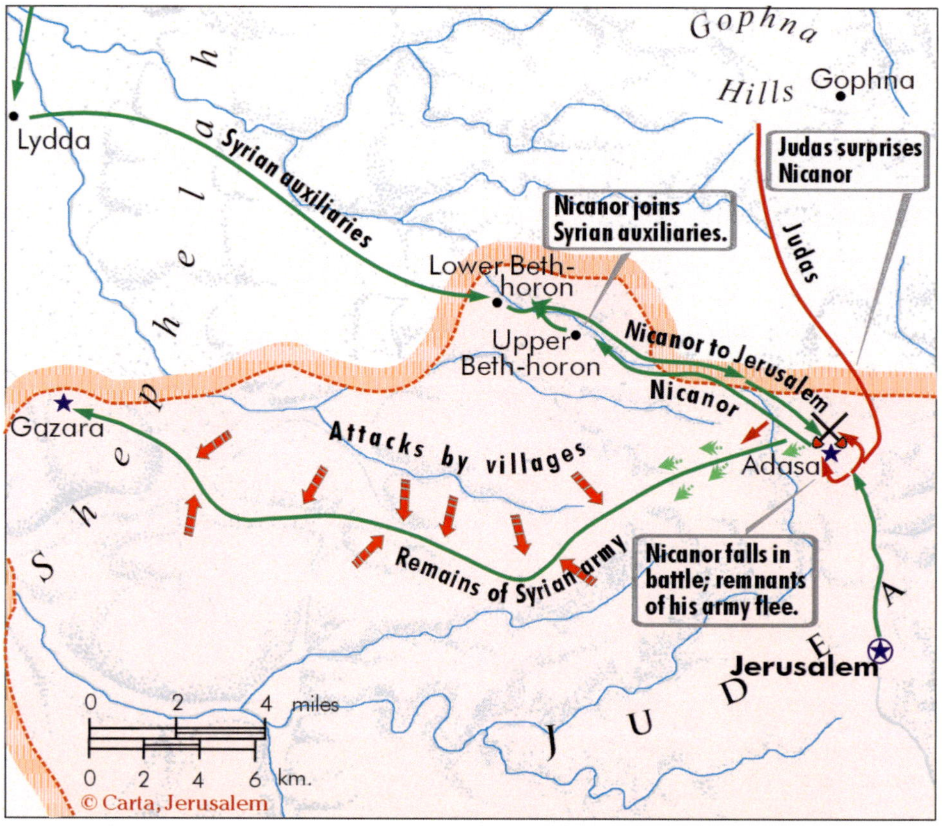

View of the Judean Desert from Masada
Author: Nehorai Mevorakh Kahalon
(Via Wikimedia Commons)

THE CAMPAIGN OF BACCHIDES
161 BCE

He sent Bacchides and Alcimus into the land of Judea the second time ...

(1 Maccabees 9:1)

Coin of Demetrius I Soter
Author: cgb.fr
(Via Wikimedia Commons)

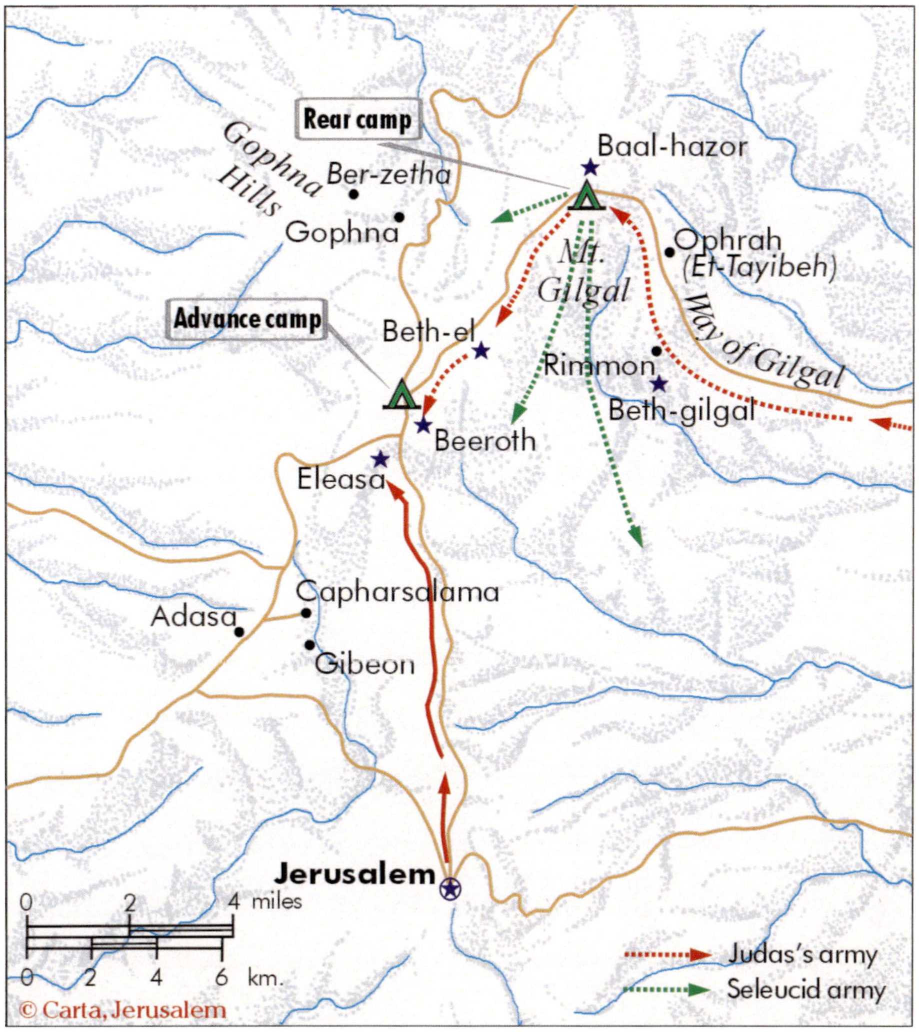

1 MACC. 9:1-4; ANT. 12:420-422

Votive relief of Hellenistic ruler Demetrius on horseback;
Fitchburg Art Museum
Author: Daderot
(Via Wikimedia Commons)

Tidings of Nicanor's defeat impelled Demetrius I again to dispatch Bacchides, with a first-class army — the so-called right wing — to Judea. The suppression of the revolt had now become urgent to the Seleucid king, for Judas in the meantime had entered into an alliance with the Romans, who were ready to support all enemies of the Seleucids. Endeavoring to surprise Judas, Bacchides, on his march from Damascus, passed through the desert and the Jordan Valley and ascended by the dangerous Gilgal route. Bacchides took vengeance on the Jewish inhabitants of "Arbela." He encamped at Eleasa, thereby cutting off both Judas and Jerusalem from the main forces of the rebels in the Gophna Hills and in the area of Modiin.

THE BATTLE OF ELEASA AND THE DEATH OF JUDAS 161 BCE

The appearance of Bacchides on the outskirts of Jerusalem surprised Judas, who had failed to realize what was happening and had not mobilized his forces in time. He was faced with three difficult choices; he could face up to the Seleucid siege of Jerusalem (with the Hellenized Jews in open support of the Syrian army), or he could retreat to the hills and abandon Jerusalem and the Temple, or he could stand and fight despite his numerical inferiority.

Judas chose the third option despite the advice of his men. The Seleucid army encamped at Beeroth (El-Bira) and Judas camped next to Eleasa (next to Ramallah). The battle took place between these two towns on a plain which was suitable to maneuvers by the cumbersome Seleucid forces. The two armies rallied against each other; on the right flank the choice troops were arrayed and were commanded by Bacchides himself on the one side and Judas on the other.

The Book of Maccabees tells us that Judas' force numbered only three thousand soldiers whereas the Seleucid force had twenty thousand infantry and two thousand cavalry. The course of battle, however, proved that Judas' army could not have been that small even though it was certainly outnumbered by the Seleucids.

Initially it seemed that Judas faired better in the battle. The Seleucid right flank began to retreat to Mt. Baal-hazor, some seven miles from the battle site, and Judas' right flank pursued them. In the second stage the battle turned. The left flank of the Seleucids split in two; one part stopped the remnants of the Jewish force and the other pulled back to aid the retreating forces. In the third stage of the battle, the retreating Seleucids managed to consolidate their ranks and thus Judas' army was captured between the two prongs of the Seleucid army. After a heroic battle the Jewish force was destroyed; Judas himself was killed.

It is difficult to understand how the retreating Seleucid force managed to organize its troops into a phalanx formation. It is therefore believed that the retreat was a ploy, in order to trap Judas' force and destroy it.

After the battle, the Jewish revolt was ostensibly crushed. Bacchides took control of Jerusalem without a battle. The remnants of the Maccabeans, with Jonathan at their head, escaped to the hills of Modiin and rekindled the flame of the revolt.

Then Judas said, God forbid that I should do this thing and flee away from them: if our time be come, let us die manfully.

(1 Maccabees 9:10)

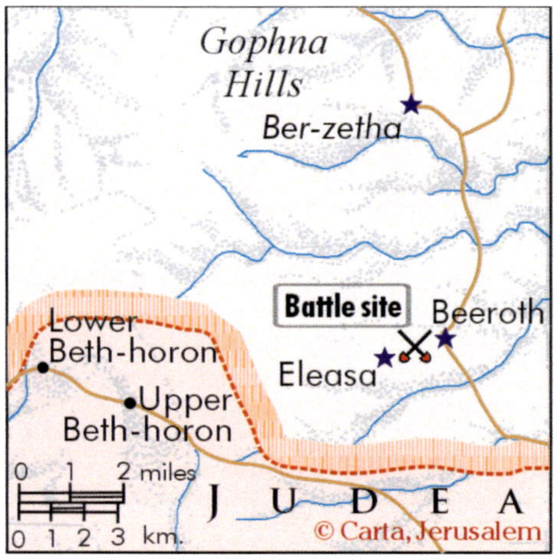

Helenistic cavalryman; painted tombstone
Carta, Jerusalem

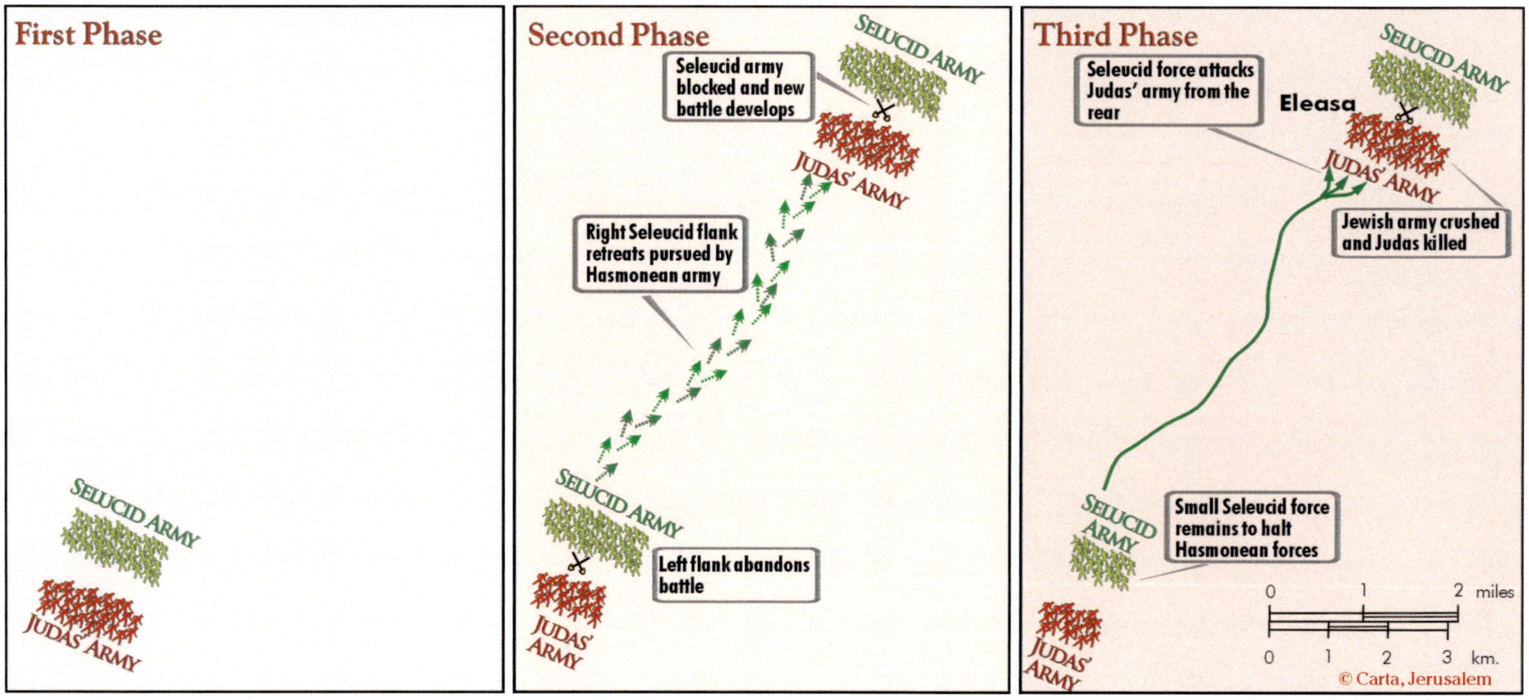

1 MACC. 9:5-19; ANT. 12:426-434

JONATHAN IN THE WILDERNESS OF JUDEA, AND THE FORTIFICATIONS OF BACCHIDES 160 TO 155 BCE

Jonathan took the governance upon him at that time, and he rose up instead of his brother Judas.

(1 Maccabees 9:31)

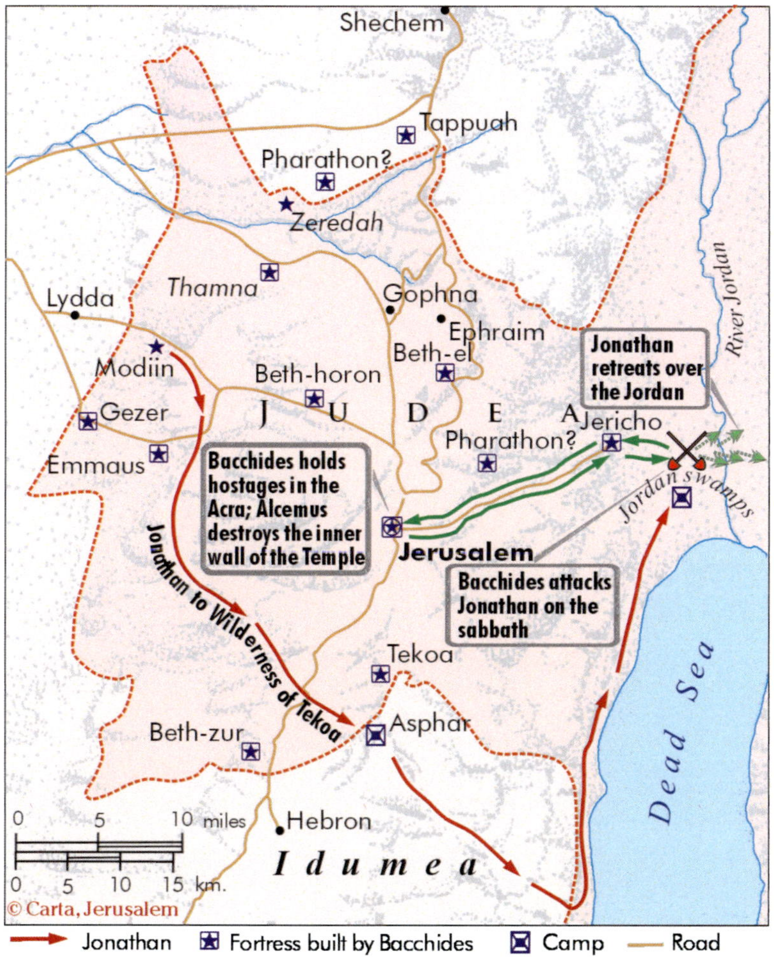

1 MACC. 9:28-33, 50; ANT. 13:5-8, 15

Judean Wilderness and the Dead Sea
Author: James Emery from Douglasville, United States
(Via Wikimedia Commons)

After the defeat at Eleasa, the Maccabeans could no longer maintain their stronghold in the mountains of Gophna. They elected Jonathan as their leader and promptly repaired to the wilderness of Tekoa, in the Judean desert, encamping near the well of Asphar.

The wilderness of Judea has served as a refuge for the oppressed and as a hideaway for insurgents since time immemorial; it was here that Jonathan rallied his supporters. It appears that Jonathan retreated and entrenched himself in the desert near Jericho on the river Jordan. Here he was confronted by Bacchides. After heavy fighting Jonathan escaped with his men by swimming across the Jordan, hoping to find sanctuary there. Before the battle with Bacchides, Jonathan had been at odds with the tribes across the Jordan and in a hostile encounter with them his brother John had been killed. Jonathan retaliated by destroying a desert caravan of one of the tribes.

To strengthen his hold on Judea, Bacchides built two tiers of fortifications, a northern and a southern line. The northern line ran north along the boundary of Judea and included Tappuah (Sheikh Abu Zarad), Tekoa according to Josephus; Pharathon (Pharan), identified by some scholars to be in the Judean desert; and Thamna. The southern line ran through the heartland of Judea and included Gezer, Emmaus, Beth-horon, Beth-el and Jericho. The area to the south was under the control of the fortress of Beth-zur. These and the royal fortresses at the Acra, Gazara and Beth-zur formed a system of defense considered adequate to safeguard rule in rebellious Judea.

Jonathan Maccabaeus, leader of the Hasmonean Dynasty 161–143 BCE
Source: "Promptuarii Iconum Insigniorum"; 1553
Author: Published by Guillaume Rouille (1518?-1589)
(Via Wikimedia Commons)

THE SIEGE OF BETH-BASI, JONATHAN AT MACHMAS 156 TO 152 BCE

Then went he and laid siege against Beth-basi; and they fought against it a long season, and made engines of war.
(1 Maccabees 9:64)

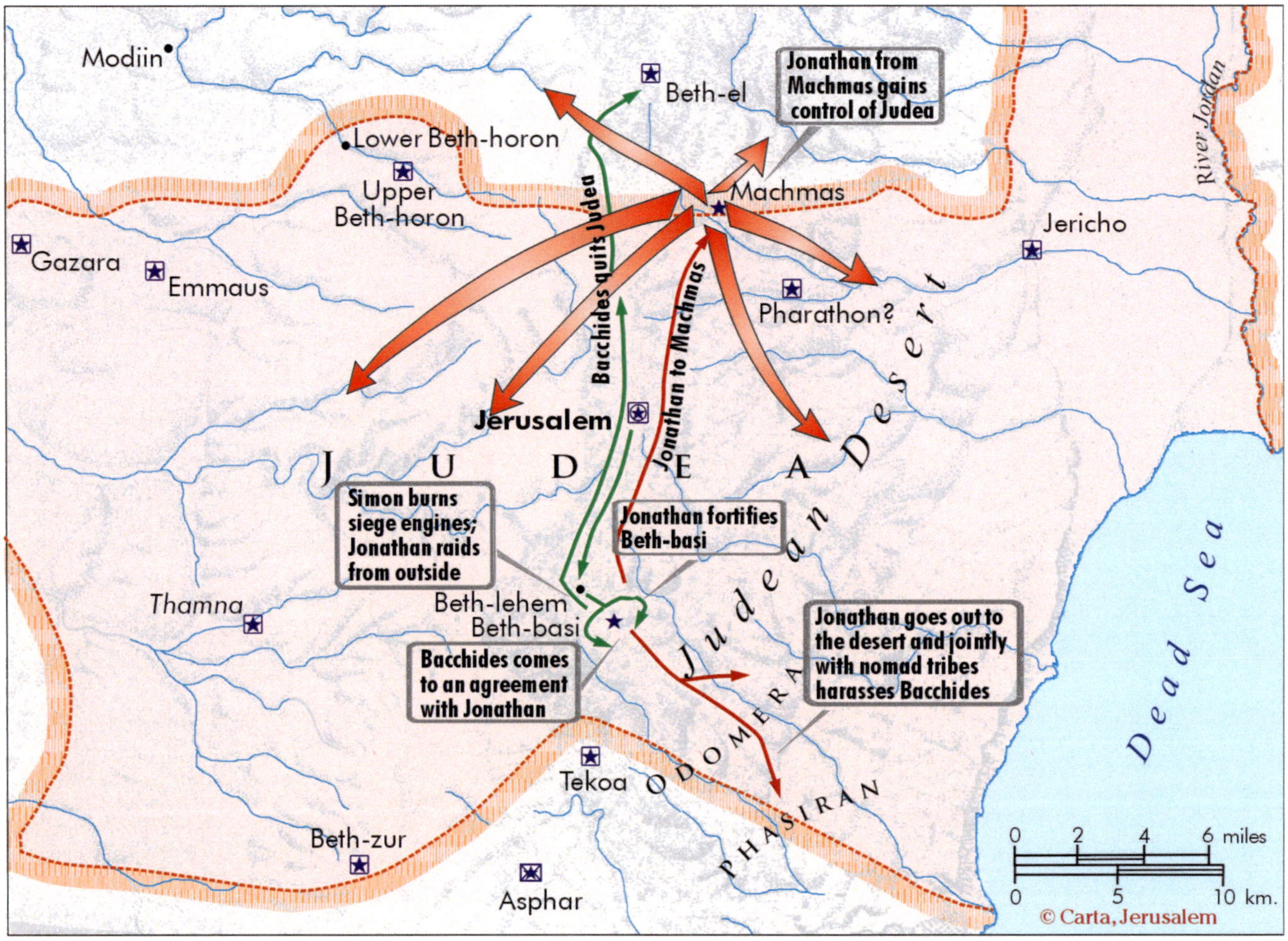

Fortress held by Bacchides — Jonathan's army — Bacchides' army

1 MACC. 9:62-73; ANT. 13:26-34

Alcimus the high priest died in 159 BCE, after he had offended the Hasidim by opening the lattice surrounding the Temple in the outer court, the limit beyond which Gentiles were not allowed to enter. Bacchides returned to Antioch, and the country remained at peace for two years. Bacchides then returned with his army, but his attempt to capture Jonathan and his men, who apparently lived in peace in Modiin, came to nothing.

The Maccabeans occupied Beth-basi, an abandoned fortress southeast of Bethlehem. This was a daring move because it occurred in a settled region, even if on the outskirts of the desert. Jonathan and his men thus gained a foothold in populated Judea, not far from the road which passes along the water divide.

Thus challenged, Bacchides assaulted Beth-basi with heavy siege machinery. Remains of the siege works were discovered near Khirbet Beth-basi in the Judean desert. Jonathan, however, was too experienced a fighter to let the enemy entrap him.

He charged his brother Simon with the defense of Beth-basi and went forth to harass Bacchides. Traveling through the desert, Jonathan came across two wandering tribes, called Odomera and Phasiran in 1 Maccabees; they are not known from any other source. Odomera resembles the name of a Bedouin tribe, the Beni Ta'amare, who live in the area of Khirbet Beth-basi to this day. Jonathan's forcefulness persuaded the tribesmen to join his attack on Bacchides. At the same time, Simon sallied forth from the city and burned the siege works. This induced Bacchides to negotiate.

The internal situation in the Seleucid kingdom had become unsettled and many plots against Demetrius I were contrived by rivals. Jonathan received permission in the agreement made, probably in 155 BCE, to settle in Machmas, while the Hellenizers continued to hold Jerusalem.

However, after Bacchides' army had left Judea, Jonathan extended his rule over the whole country, except for the capital and the fortress of Beth-zur: "And (Jonathan) began to govern the people; and he destroyed the ungodly men out of Israel" (1 Macc. 9:73).

THE EXPANSION OF JUDEA IN THE DAYS OF JONATHAN 152 TO 142 BCE

And sent him a buckle of gold, as the use is to be given to such as are of the king's blood: he gave him also Accaron with the borders thereof in possession.
(1 Maccabees 10:89)

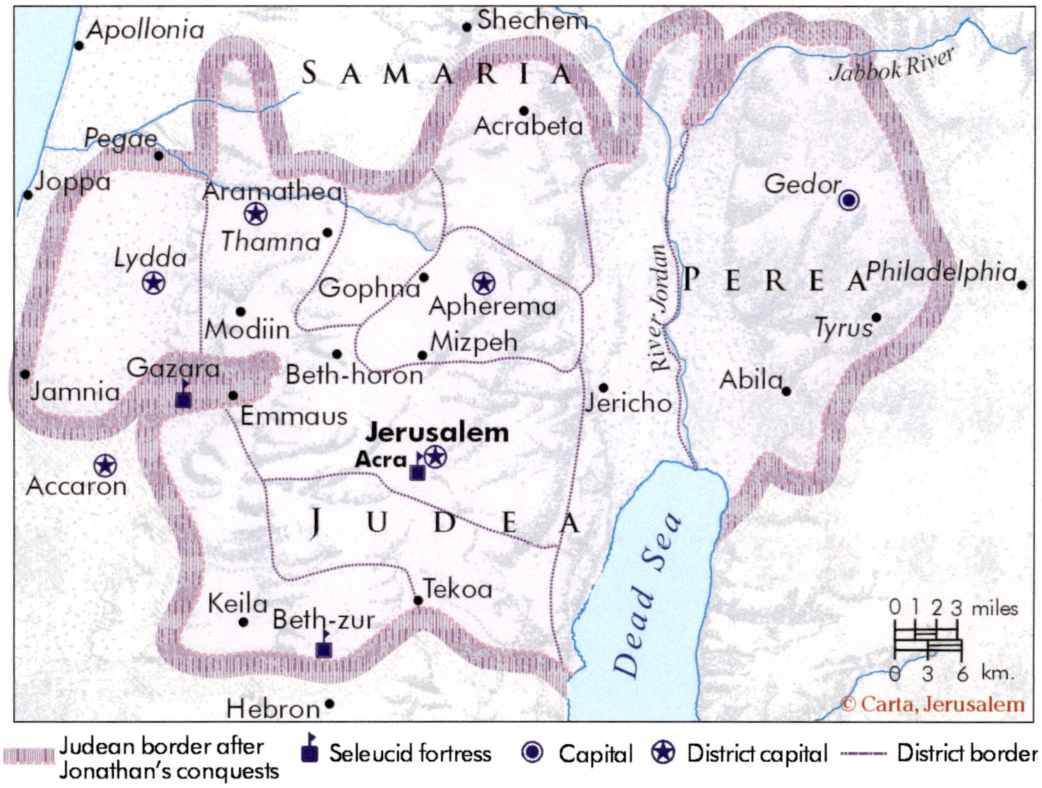

Jonathan exploited the decline of Seleucid rule to raise the prestige of Judea. When Demetrius I learned that Alexander Balas, who claimed to be the son of Antiochus IV, had invaded Ptolemais, he felt endangered and granted Jonathan the privileges of a royally appointed commander. He permitted the Hasmonean to recruit an army and to forge weapons. He also returned the Jewish hostages held in the Acra. These concessions enabled Jonathan to establish himself in Jerusalem and repair the fortifications of the Temple Mount. Except for the Acra and Beth-zur, Jonathan was the de facto ruler of Judea.

Alexander Balas, who also wanted Jonathan's support, appointed him high priest. Jonathan wore the finery of this office for the first time during the feast of Tabernacles in the year 152 BCE Demetrius in turn tempted Jonathan by offering him the three districts with Jewish populations, still under the administration of Samaria. Jonathan, however, supported Alexander, the weaker of the two rivals; and Alexander defeated Demetrius I in 150 BCE

At a meeting in Ptolemais between Alexander and Ptolemy VI in the same year, Jonathan was also present and the Syrian king granted him the title "Strategos and Meridarches" (commander and governor) of Judea. After Jonathan had overcome the forces of Demetrius II in the battle of Jamnia, Alexander gave him the district of Accaron as an estate (147 BCE). Demetrius II then also realized that it was preferable to have Jonathan as an ally rather than an enemy and approved the transfer of three districts (Lydda, Aramathea, and Apherema) from Samaria to Judea. When Tryphon, regent for Antiochus VI, rose against Demetrius II, he too wished to remain in the good graces of Jonathan and, in 144 BCE, endorsed his annexation of the "four districts." From the phrasing of the endorsement we can infer that Jonathan had meanwhile added the Perea — Jewish "Transjordan" — a legacy from the Tobiads, to his dominions: it is possible that the fourth district was Accaron or Acrabeta.

Hasmonean burial chamber, showing the typical niches and ossuaries.
Source: Jewish Tomb at Dominus Flavit
Author: Ian Scott
(Via Wikimedia Commons)

THE FIRST CONQUEST OF JOPPA AND THE BATTLE OF JAMNIA
147 BCE

And east darts at the people, from morning till evening. But the people stood still, as Jonathan had commanded them and so the enemies' horses were tired.

(1 Maccabees 10:80-81)

In 147 BCE, when Demetrius II had triumphed over his rival Alexander Balas, he appointed one Apollonius as commander of Coele-Syria and instructed him to take strong measures against Judea, which had supported Alexander Balas. Apollonius, encamped at Jamnia, challenged Jonathan to a contest "in the valley, where there is no stone, no rock, no place to flee to." He believed that the Jewish army could win only by irregular warfare in the mountains. But the Maccabean army had grown stronger and Jonathan, at the head of ten thousand men, went to war in the plain, joined by Simon and a further battalion. As a start to their campaign, the Maccabeans forced Joppa to open its gates to them.

Apollonius had meanwhile prepared an ambush between Jamnia and Azotus. He concealed a regiment of horsemen along the road between the two towns and feigned a retreat. Jonathan followed him and when the two armies clashed, the Jewish forces were attacked from the rear. In the ensuing battle the Jewish army proved its prowess; "the people" stood fast for a whole day until the enemies' horses wearied. At eventide Simon attacked the cavalry, who fled toward the coast. The remainder of Apollonius' army retreated to Azotus, with Jonathan pursuing them. Azotus was captured, and the Jewish force proceeded to Ascalon, which received Jonathan cordially.

The Maccabean army emerged from the battle as the strongest military power in the whole Land of Israel. According to the description of the battle, the Jewish military force was organized in a phalanx formation and included cavalry.

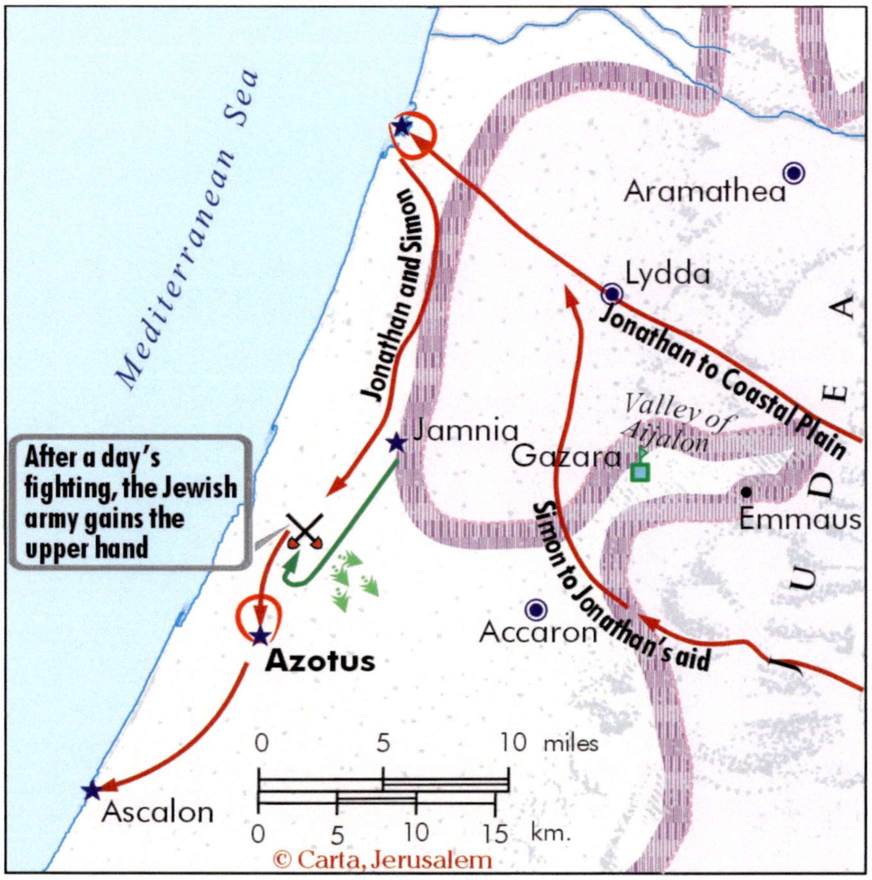

1 MACC. 10:69-87; ANT. 13:88-101

Greek inscription on chalkstone from the Hasmonean period, from Jamnia; Archaeological Museum Beit Miriam, Kibbutz Palmahim; Author: Hanay (Via Wikimedia Commons)

THE CAMPAIGN OF JONATHAN IN COELE-SYRIA
150 BCE

Afterward Jonathan returned to Jerusalem with peace and gladness.
(1 Maccabees 10:66)

The position of Demetrius II was further weakened when he dismissed his Cretan mercenaries. The king was forced to seek the aid of Jonathan in suppressing Tryphon's rebellion. Jonathan sent three thousand men to defend Demetrius from the Antiochian mob besieging him in his palace. The Jews gained the upper hand and — for a time — saved the throne of Demetrius II. The latter, as soon as he felt himself secure, forgot his promises to Jonathan.

Meanwhile, the power of Tryphon and Antiochus VI increased steadily. To win Jonathan's support, Tryphon appointed Simon royal governor of the coastal plain, from the Ladder of Tyre to the Brook of Egypt. Jonathan and his army passed through the whole region of Coele-Syria at their pleasure, arrived once more at Ascalon, and there were received with great pomp. The residents of Gaza, however, kept their gates shut. Jonathan devastated the outskirts of the city and forced the citizens to conclude a treaty with him. Again Jonathan crossed the country to Damascus. At the same time, Simon captured Beth-zur. In all Judea, only the Acra of Jerusalem remained in alien hands.

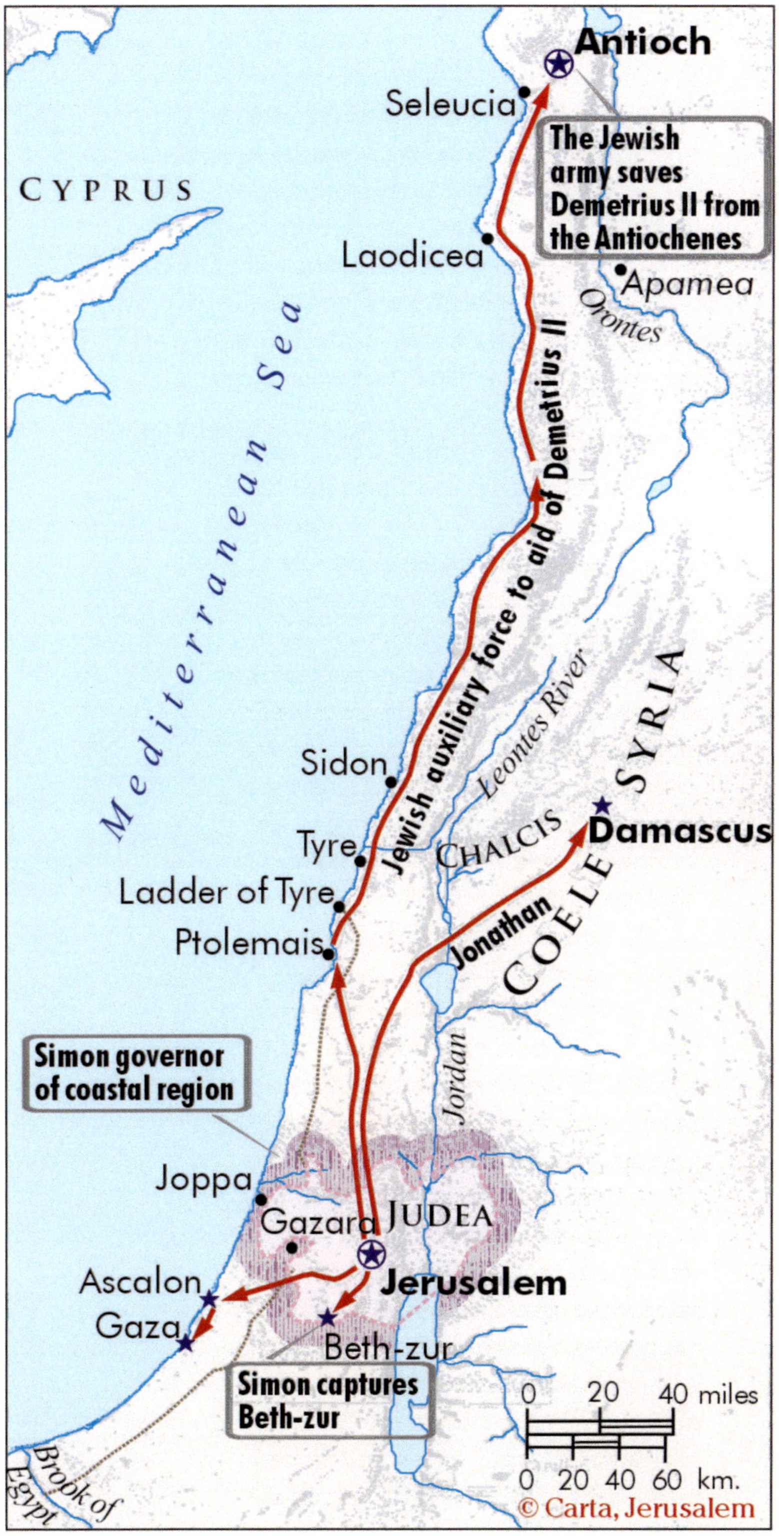

1 MACC. 10:57-65; ANT. 13:103-105, 133-142, 146, 148-153

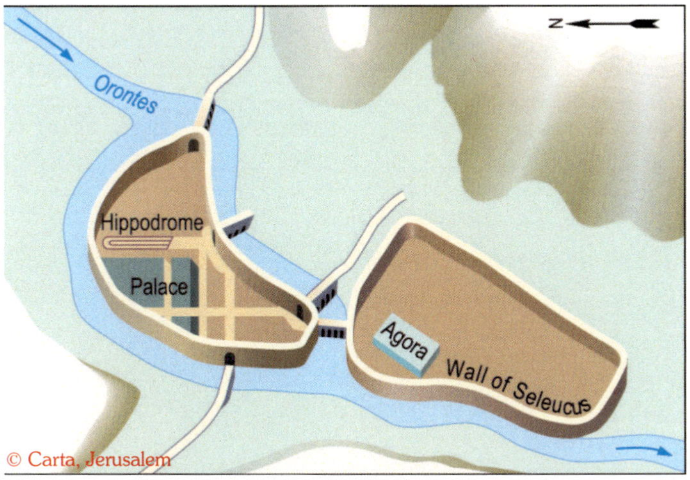

Plan of Antioch in the Hellenistic period; Carta, Jerusalem

Cardo Maximus, Apamea, Orontes River Valley, North-West Syria
Author: James Gordon from Los Angeles, California, USA
(Via Wikimedia Commons)

THE BATTLE OF HAZOR 144 BCE

The daring exploits of Jonathan in Coele-Syria made Demetrius' commanders suspicious that, in theory at least, Jonathan was acting for his rival, Antiochus VI. To curb his activities, Demetrius' troops advanced beyond Damascus and camped at Cadasa on the boundary of Galilee. Jonathan left Gennesaret and went up to the plain of Hazor (near ancient Hazor). Demetrius' generals again tried the ruse used by Apollonius at Jamnia. They hid part of their army in the hills of Cadasa and attacked Jonathan from the rear after he had joined battle with the main force. A large part of the Maccabean army panicked; only Jonathan and his generals, Mattathias son of Absalom and Judas son of Hilphai, stood fast and finally defeated the enemy, chasing them to Cadasa and capturing their camp.

"The Maccabees Resist the Syrians—Siege and Destruction", 1888
Authors: Rawson, Albert L. (Albert Leighton), 1829-1902
Hagar, George J. (George Jotham), 1847-1921
(Via Wikimedia Commons)

Afterward turning again to battle, he put them to fight, and so they ran away.
(1 Maccabees 11:72)

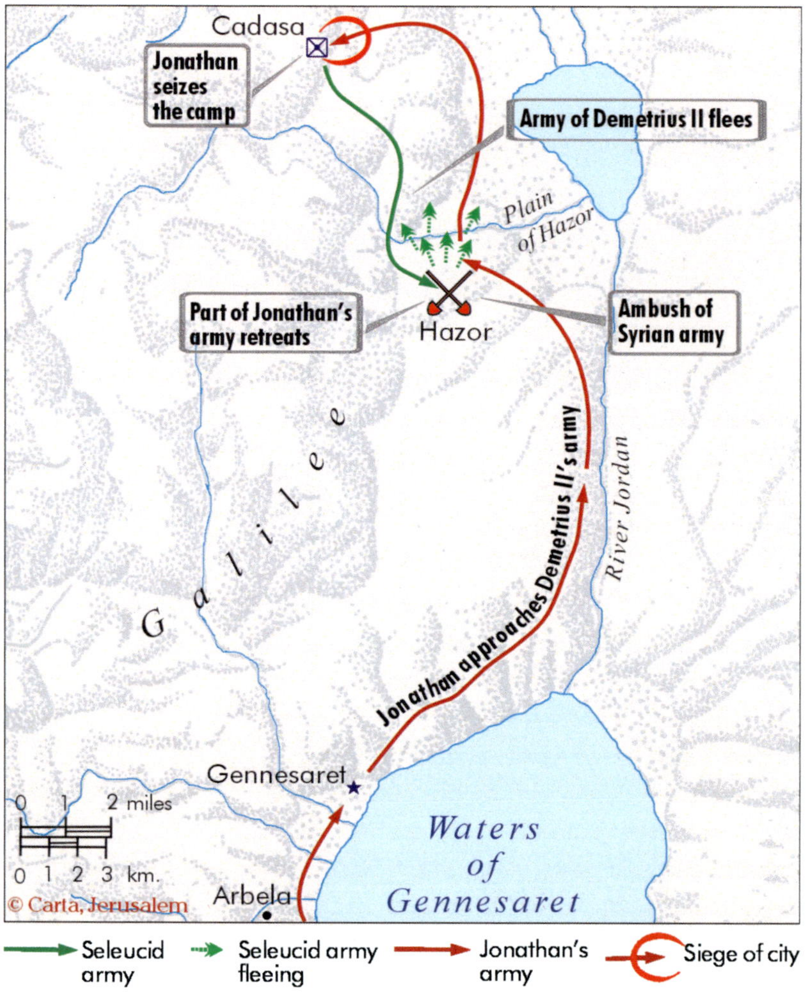

1 MACC. 11:63-74; ANT. 13:158-162

Tel Hazor, Citadel and archaeological site
Author: Qasinka
(Via Wikimedia Commons)

THE HAMATH CAMPAIGN 143 BCE

On the seventeenth (day of Adar) the Gentiles arose against the remainder of the scribes in the country of Chalcis and Beth-zabdai; and there was a salvation for the children of Israel.
(Scroll of Fasting)

Jonathan felt the tide turning in his favor and sent delegations to Rome and Sparta to renew old alliances. Again the armies of Demetrius started out against him, but for once the fight did not take place in the Land of Israel, for Jonathan "gave them no opportunity to come into the land" (1 Macc. 12:25). The armies deployed in the district of Hamath in the valley of Lebanon. When Demetrius' armies saw no chance to defeat Jonathan they secretly retired across the river Eleutherus, which marked the boundary of Coele-Syria. Jonathan turned toward Beth-zabdai, in the land of Chalcis (where the remnants of the Jewish population were being persecuted), freed his brethren and took booty from the enemy. From there he proceeded to Damascus and crossed the breadth of Coele-Syria. Simon had meanwhile captured Joppa for the second time, and fortified Adida, overlooking the coastal highway near Lydda.

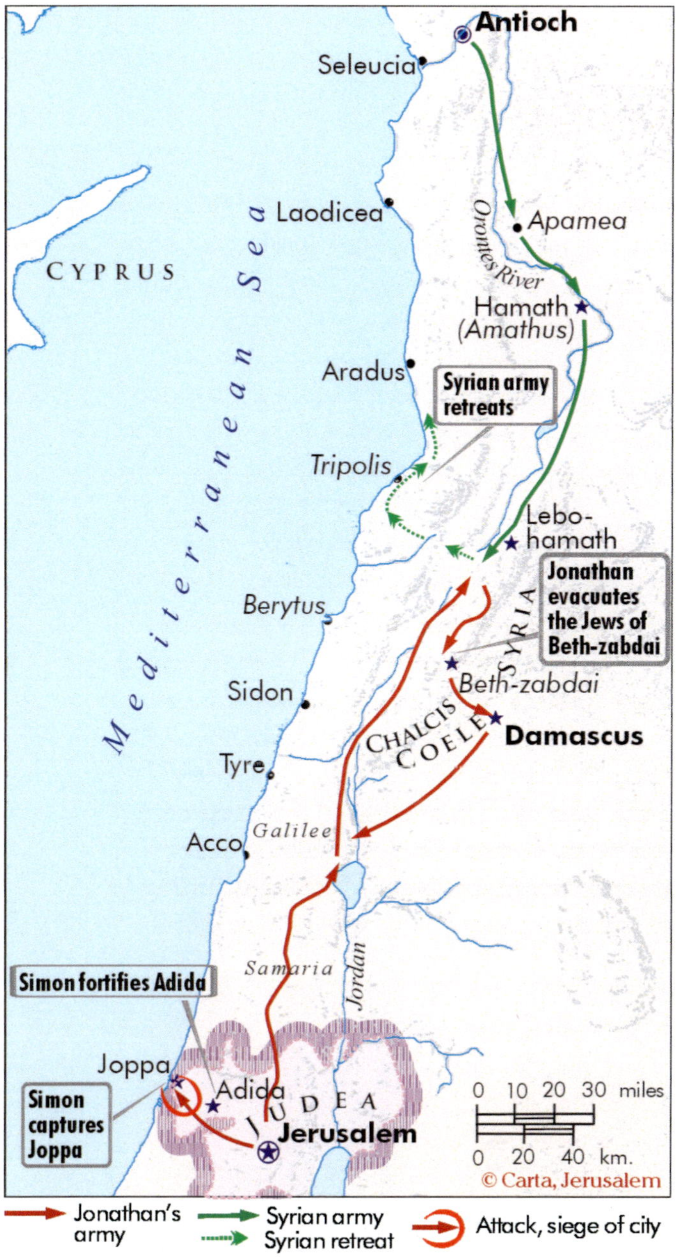

"Twelve Leaves" symbol of Hellenism
Author: Nyo
(Via Wikimedia Commons)

1 MACC. 12:24-32, 38; ANT. 13:174-180

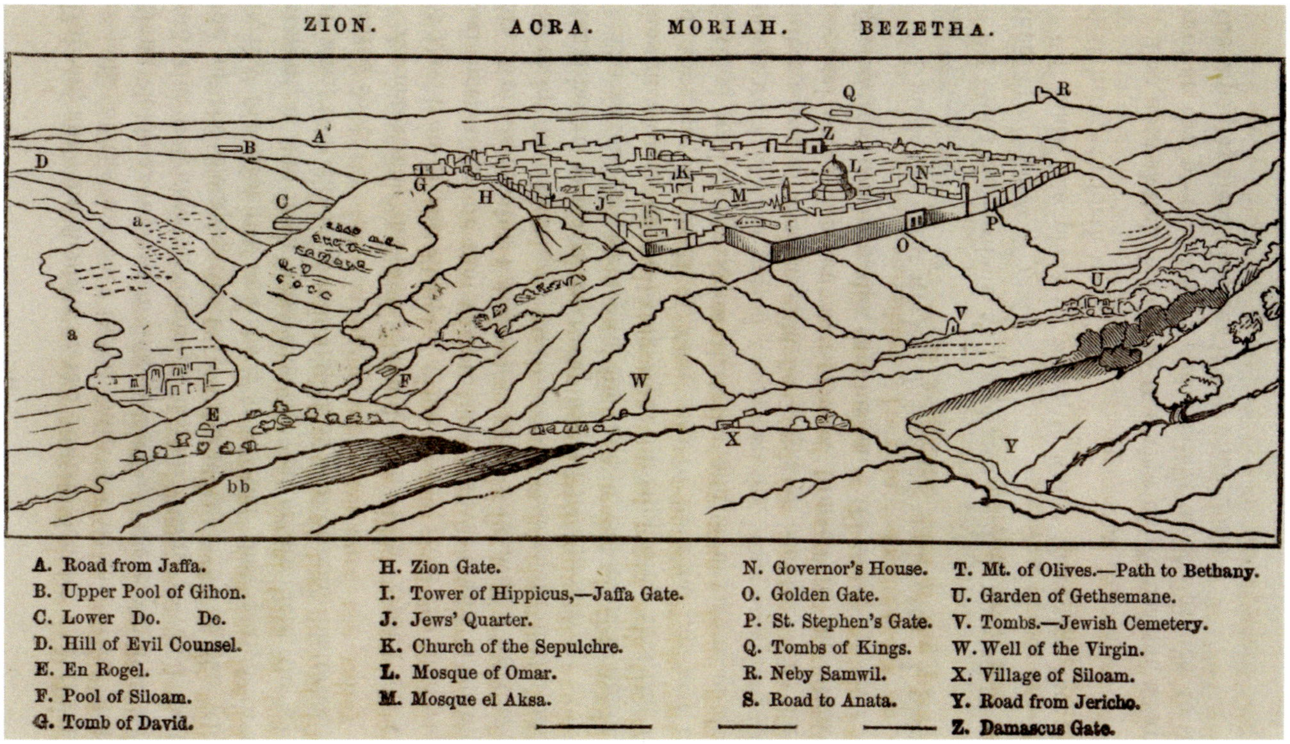

"Modern Jerusalem" from The Gems of Masonry, 1859
Author: Sherer, John
(Via Wikimedia Commons)

JERUSALEM OF THE MACCABEES 164 TO 141 BCE

At the beginning of Hellenization, the more "progressive" citizens felt that the old city on the eastern hill, surrounded by ancient walls (restored by Nehemiah, and again in the days of Antiochus III), was hardly fit to be the new "Antiochia." They probably decided to build a city in the Hippodamic tradition: straight streets intersecting at right angles. They started to construct this city on the western hill between the valley of Hinnom and the Tyropoeon valley. A hillock at the eastern end of this new Hellenistic city, protected by a small valley to the west, served as its fortress. In the Maccabean period it was called Acra — not to be confused with the old Acra, the citadel (Baris) of the days of Nehemiah, which was situated north of the Temple Mount. (There have been several suggestions as to the location of the Acra.)

With the capture by Judas Maccabeus of the Temple Mount and the renewal of worship in the Temple, in 164 BCE, the city was divided into two parts, a division which lasted until 141 BCE The Maccabeans held Mount Zion in the days of Judas, and again in the days of Jonathan and Simon — always in opposition to the Hellenizers' fortress. By raising a siege wall, the "Caphenatha," and rebuilding a quarter named after it, Jonathan and Simon tried to cut off the garrison of the Acra from the marketplace (the Hellenistic "Agora") and to force its surrender through starvation.

After the final conquest of the Acra in 141 BCE, the Jews razed the part of the fortress commanding the Temple (Ant. 13:217). The Maccabeans, now lords of the entire city, built a wall around the western hill, constructed a bridge across the Tyropoeon valley, between the Temple Mount and the western hill, and built a palace for themselves on the ruins of the Acra. They also strengthened the "Citadel" by adding towers, one of which was called Strato's Tower in the days of Aristobulus I.

Let Jerusalem also be holy and free ...
(1 Maccabees 10:31)

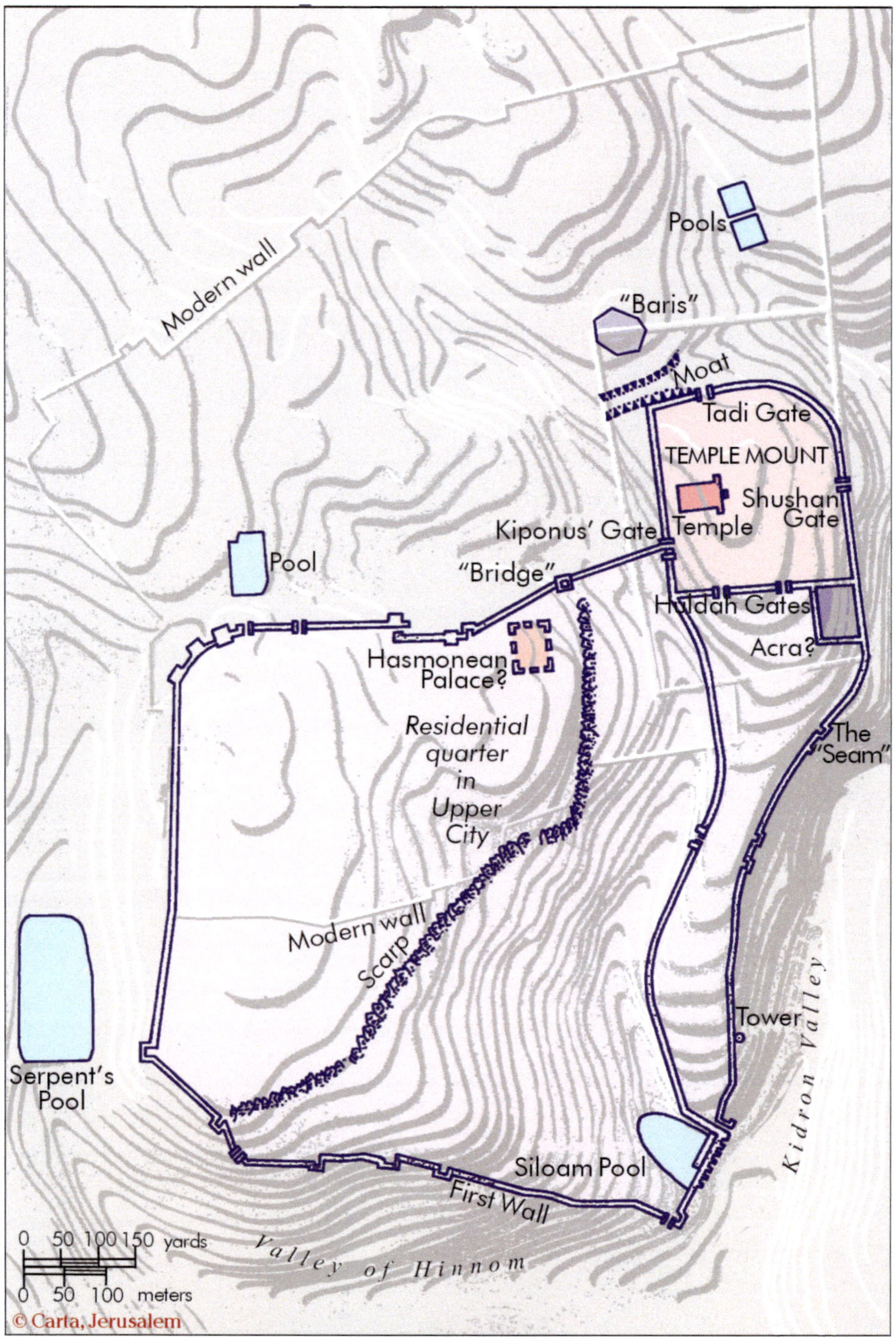

1 MACC. 4:37-60; 6:61-62; 10:10-12; 12:36-37; 13:49-53

Left: Southern Wall of the Temple Mount enclosure and stairs leading to the triple Hulda gates.
To the left of the stairs: Hellenistic or Hasmonean remains attributed to the Seleucid Acra.
Author: Oren Rozen
(Via Wikimedia Commons)

TRYPHON'S CAMPAIGN AGAINST JONATHAN 143 TO 142 BCE

And they answered with a loud voice, saying, Thou shalt be our leader instead of Judas and Jonathan thy brother.
(1 Maccabees 13:8)

When Tryphon had the upper hand (while his rival Demetrius II was occupied with the preparation of his campaign against the Parthians) he decided to cut Jonathan down to size, the ruler of Judea seemingly having become too independent. Tryphon and his army set out for Judea, but Jonathan met him at Beth-shean with so strong a force that it was obvious to the Seleucid regent that he could not overcome the Jews in battle. Tryphon therefore decided to ensnare Jonathan by leading him on with promises of turning over Ptolemais, the royal fortress. He persuaded Jonathan to send home most of his forces, which he did but for a guard of three thousand. Both men marched toward the coast. Near Ptolemais, Jonathan was induced to leave an additional two thousand men in western Galilee and Esdraelon (where Jewish settlement had apparently been renewed). Thus, only one thousand men accompanied him to within Ptolemais. The inhabitants, who had conspired with Tryphon, closed the gates of the city and slaughtered the Jewish troops; thus Jonathan was taken captive by his enemies.

Tryphon wished to exploit the confusion now reigning among the Jews, in order to subdue them, but his attack on Jonathan's troops remaining in Galilee was repelled, and Simon assumed command and encouraged the dejected people. Tryphon then went up against Judea, with Jonathan a prisoner in his camp. Simon ordered his general, Jonathan son of Absalom, to capture Joppa and resettle it with Jews. He then positioned his army near the new fortress of Adida. Tryphon dared not meet the Jewish army face to face, but tried Lysias' old ruse: he passed through Idumea near Adora to the road along the watershed. The Hellenizers beleaguered in the Acra, in their despair, called for his help and Tryphon tried to reach Jerusalem in a forced march through the Judean desert. Caught by a snowstorm, however, he was forced to retreat to the warmth of the Jordan Valley.

After his failure, Tryphon returned by way of Gilead, putting Jonathan to death at Bascama (Beth-shikma). Jonathan was buried with great pomp in the family tomb in Modiin. Simon was elected to lead the people in his brother's stead.

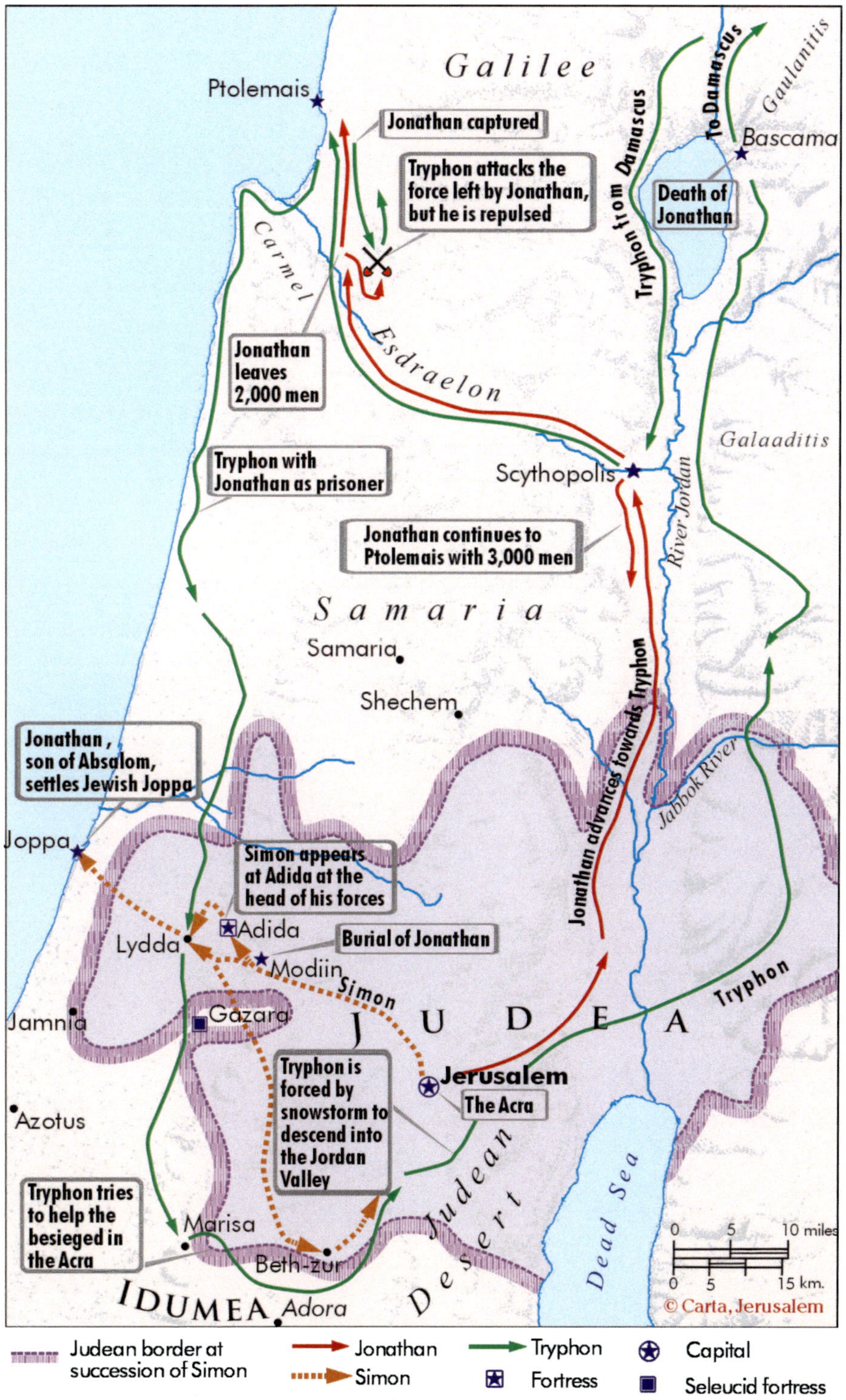

1 MACC. 12:39-53; 13:1-30; ANT. 13:187-212

Cavalry and infantry battle
(On a sarcophagus from Sidon)
Carta, Jerusalem

THE CONQUESTS OF SIMON 142 TO 135 BCE

Then did they till their ground in peace ...
(1 Maccabees 14:8)

Tryphon's treachery drove Simon to side with Demetrius II, who granted independence to Judea in 142 BCE. Now "the yoke of the foreigners was removed from Israel, and the people began to write: 'In the first year of Simon the high priest ...' "

But Simon was not satisfied with Judean independence within its existing boundaries. Already in the days of Tryphon he had added Joppa: "He took Joppa for a harbor and made it an entrance to the islands of the sea." He also took Gazara (Gezer) with the aid of a siege machine (helepolis), and then built there a fortress and a palace, and turned the city into a Jewish military center second only to Jerusalem. And finally, he forced the people of the Acra to surrender, and "a great enemy was annihilated in Israel."

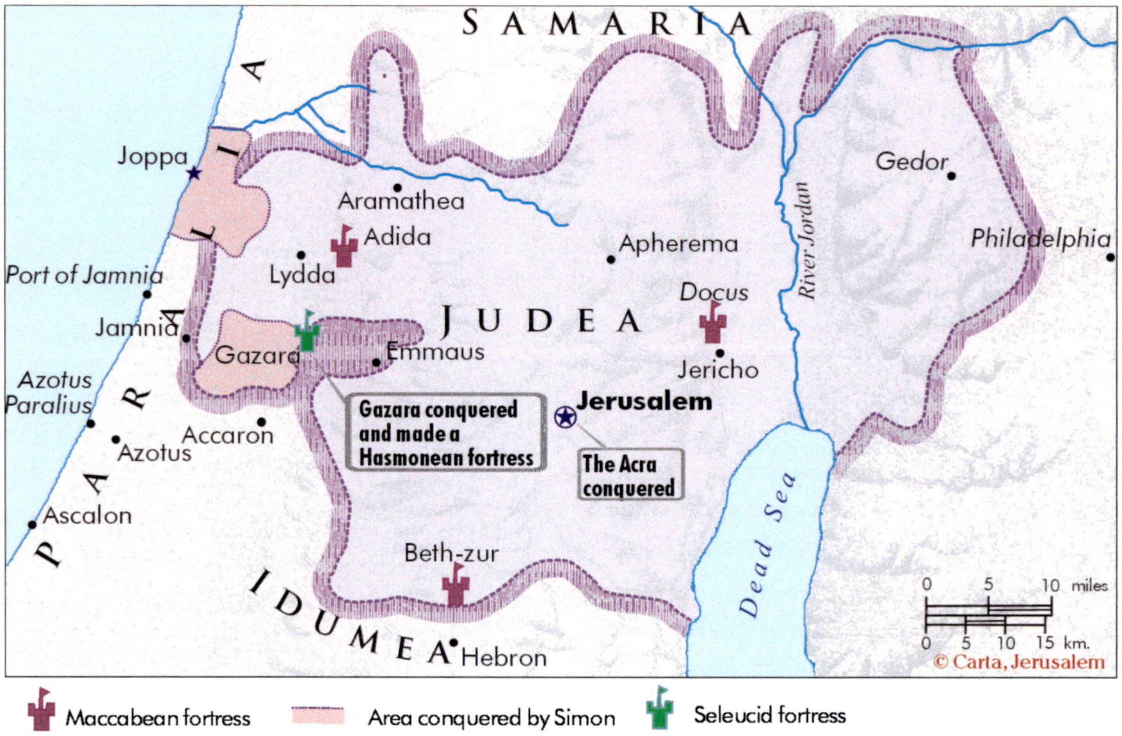

1 MACC. 13:42-48, 14:5; ANT. 13:215; WAR 1:50

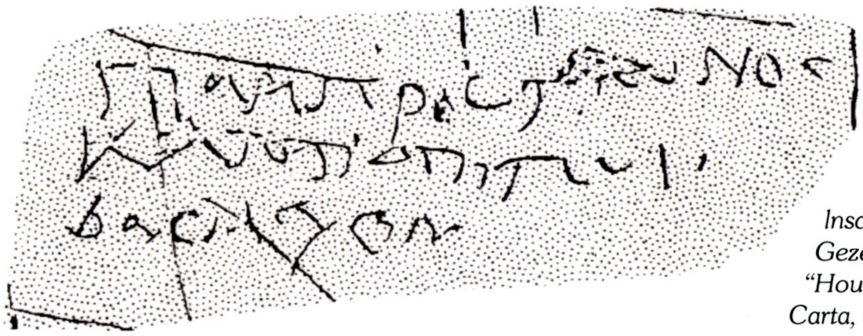

Inscription from Gezer (Gazara) cursing the "House of Simon" Carta, Jerusalem

Gezer-Stone steles
(GNU Free Documentation License; from: Wikimedia Commons)

THE BATTLE OF KIDRON
137 BCE

In 137 BCE, Antiochus VII succeeded in evicting the pretender Tryphon from Dora. He now found himself in Judea with a strong army and tried to wrest from Simon the districts that, in his opinion, the Jews held unlawfully — in particular, Joppa and Gazara. The Seleucid king appointed his general, Cendebeus, as commander of the "Paralia" district and put at his disposal both mounted and foot soldiers. Cendebeus was ordered to build a fortress at Kidron (near modern Gedera) on the Judean border. He then transferred his headquarters to Jamnia, whence he proceeded to harass the population of Judea.

To counter this new danger, John Hyrcanus, the son of Simon, moved to Gazara, facing Kidron. From there John and Judas, his brother, went forth with twenty thousand soldiers to surprise the Seleucid forces (passing a night in Modiin). At dawn they advanced to Kidron until only the river in the lower part of the valley of Sorek separated the opposing forces.

The Seleucids were deployed in their usual manner — infantry in the center and horse flanking. However, John — with little cavalry — scattered his horses among his foot soldiery. In spite of the difficult terrain, which required crossing the river, the Maccabeans prevailed; the Syrians fled, first to Kidron and later to forts in the territory of Azotus. Judas was wounded at Kidron, but John doggedly pursued his enemy to Azotus and destroyed the forts there.

Simon was not for long to enjoy the victory of his sons; Ptolemy son of Abubus, his own son-in-law, whom he had appointed as governor of Jericho, treacherously killed him together with his sons Judas and Mattathias, during a banquet at Docus (135 BCE). But the murderer's scheme, to hand Judea over to Antiochus VII, failed. John Hyrcanus, who at the time was at the fortress of Gazara, escaped the assassin. Thus perished Simon, the last surviving of Mattathias' five sons — none of whom died a natural death.

This brings to a close the history of the Hasmoneans in the first book of Maccabees. It is written there (16:23-24):

> "As concerning the rest of the acts of John, and his wars ... behold, these are written in the chronicles of his priesthood ...";

but this latter book has not come down to us. From here on we rely upon Josephus' Antiquities as the main source of Jewish history.

He himself advanced with his force in another direction ... came through without losing a single engagement.
(Antiquities 13:227)

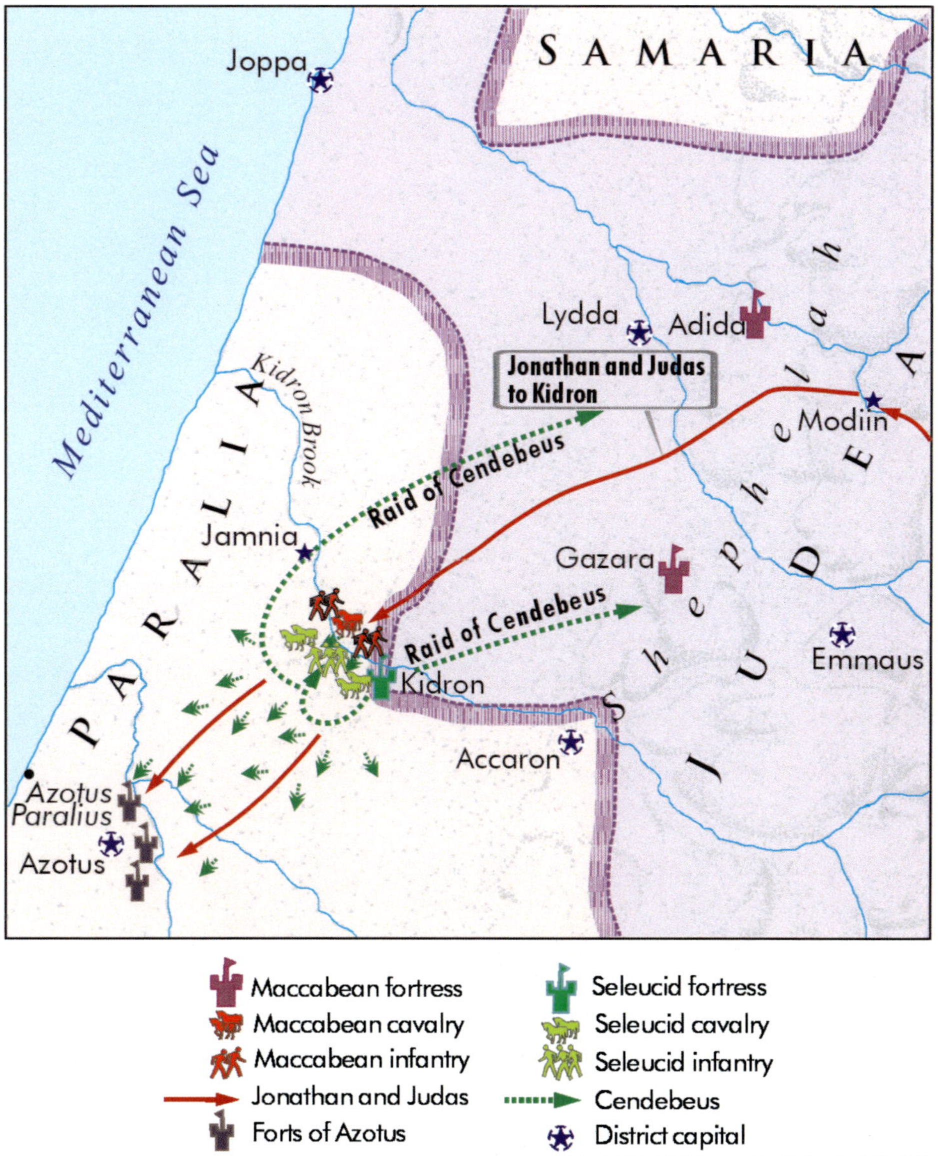

1 MACC. 15:38-16:10; ANT. 13:223-235

A coin of the last major Seleucid king, Antiochus VII (138-129 BCE), from the Christus Gardens collection in Gatlinburg, Tennessee. Author: Mary Harrsch (Via Wikimedia Commons)

THE CONQUESTS OF HYRCANUS BEYOND THE JORDAN
128 BCE

In 129 BCE Antiochus VII was killed warring against the Parthians. With his death, the power of the once mighty Seleucid dynasty came virtually to an end.

Hyrcanus was now completely free from the interference of Syria. His army was the most powerful in the region, and he began to reacquire what he considered to be the patrimony of the Israelites from the days of David.

His first conquests were beyond the Jordan near Perea, where the Jews had had a foothold since the days of Jonathan and the Tobiads. Hyrcanus attacked Medeba and captured it after a prolonged siege; he then took Samaga, a town in the region of Esbus.

With this, the Maccabeans acquired a strong position straddling the "King's highway," the important international route from Aila on the Red Sea to Damascus following the edge of the desert. This, together with possession of a section of the coastal route between Lydda and Pegae, gave Hyrcanus control of the two major commercial routes crossing the Land of Israel.

Hasmonean coin of John Hyrcanus I (Yehohanan). 135-104 BCE. showing a double cornucopiae adorned with ribbons; and a pomegranate between the horns. Source: CNG coins Author: CNG (Via Wikimedia Commons)

And he captured Medeba ... next he captured Samaga ...
(Antiquities 13:255)

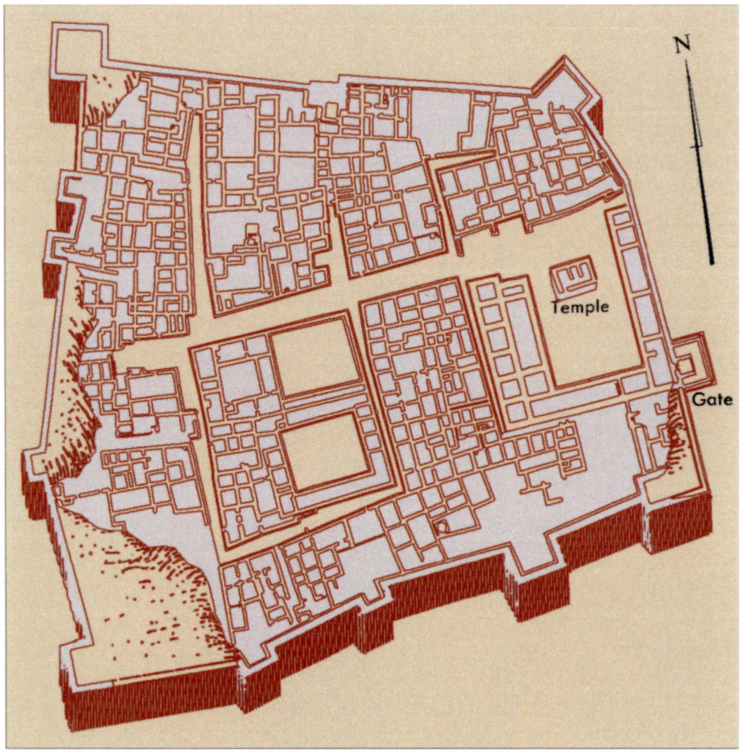

Plan of Hellenistic Marisa
Carta, Jerusalem

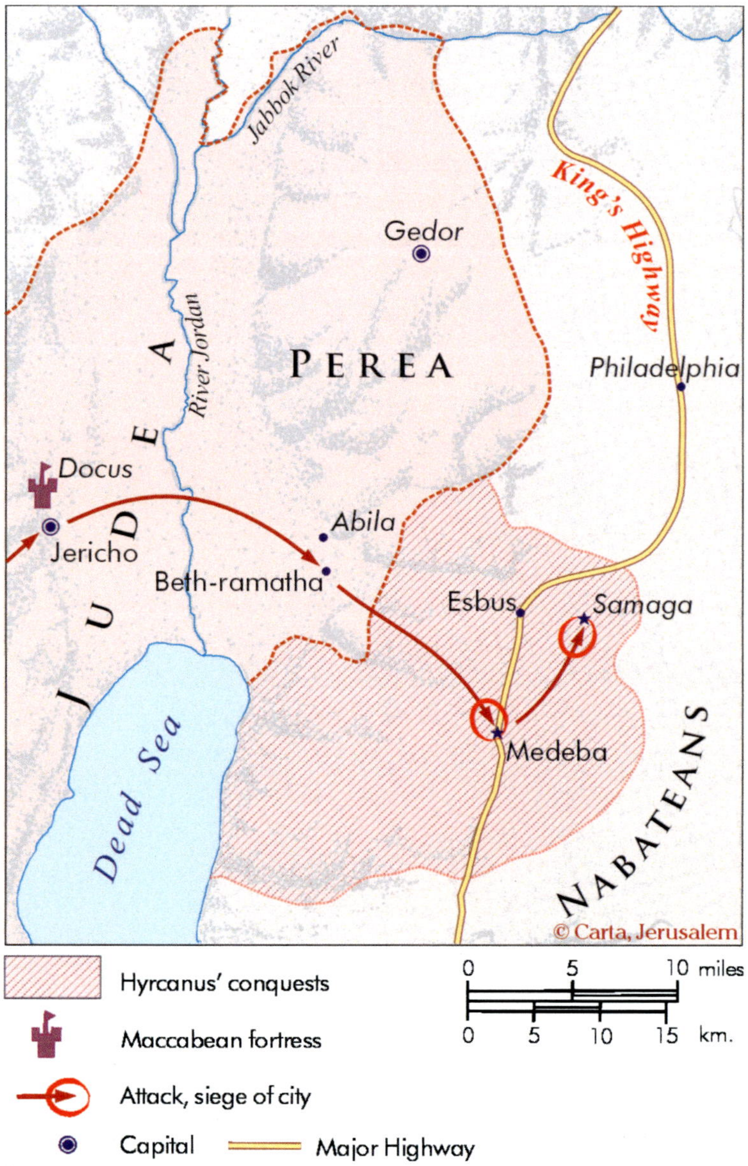

ANT. 13:255; WAR 1:63

John Hyrcanus, 1553
Source: "Promptuarii Iconum Insigniorum"
Author: Published by Guillaume Rouille (1518?-1589)
(Via Wikimedia Commons)

THE MAIN HIGHWAYS IN THE ANCIENT EAST

The main highways played a most important part in the history of the Holy Land. The settlements of Palestine are located at the crossroads of the Ancient East. The most important route was the highway from Mesopotamia to Egypt, and on it were founded the important political centers. From earliest times commercial caravans plied the major highways, carrying their products, precious objects, and luxuries; and providing for the needs of the caravans and their security, became a constant source of income. These ways, however, were not open for trade and commerce alone: military campaigns and conquests also trod them throughout history, leaving in their wake destruction and desolation. In most periods the Holy Land was dominated by major foreign powers, northern or southern, who mainly strove to secure a hold on these routes.

The mountainous nature of the Palestinian terrain dictates the courses of the roads. The principal international route connecting Egypt with North Syria and Mesopotamia transverses the Southern Levant from south to north, following the line of the seacoast in the south until reaching the barrier of Nahal Kanah (Nahr el-Auja) where it had to swerve eastward to go around Aphek.

It then skirted the eastern edge of the northern Sharon Plain and passed to the Jezreel Valley either via the valley of Aruna to Megiddo or via the valley of Dothan. From there it most probably went past Beth-shean, either north to Hazor and the Lebanese Beqa or across the Jordan to Damascus. The segment from Egypt across Sinai was called "the Way of the god Horus" by the Egyptians and once it was called "way of the land of the Philistines" (Exod. 13:17). Apart from that, this great international trunk route has no name either in the Bible or in extra-biblical sources, Roman or otherwise.

The second international route was the highway (Num. 21:22), which passes through the hill-country of Transjordan, close to the desert. This is the secondary route from Damascus to Egypt, its importance lying in the fact that the roads to Arabia branch off from it. There existed various other secondary, local roads, which were used largely by local traffic, and in time of need they also served as alternatives for international trade caravans. The map shows only the more important routes, especially those mentioned by name in the Bible.

We will go up by the highway; and if we drink of your water, I and my cattle, then I will pay for it...
(Numbers 20:19)

Camel caravan in the desert.
Author: Yoavd
(Via Wikimedia Commons)

THE CONQUESTS OF HYRCANUS IN IDUMEA 112 BCE

Hyrcanus next turned against two small peoples isolated between emerging Judea and the Greek cities: the Samaritans and the Idumeans.

The latter had previously lived in southern Transjordan, but were drawn to the fertile parts of southern Judea following the depopulation brought about by the exile under Nebuchadnezzar. These Idumeans had lost contact with their Arab neighbors and offered little resistance. Their conquest gained Hyrcanus Hebron and Adora. The semi-Hellenized Marisa was completely destroyed.

According to Josephus, the Idumeans were forced to convert to Judaism in order to assure their loyalty; but some scholars nowadays doubt whether in fact the Idumeans were converted forcibly or by choice. In any event, within a few generations they were integrated into the Jewish nation, as witnessed by their great bravery in the war against the Romans. The conquest of Idumea extended the borders of Judea to Beer-sheba and Orda.

He further took numerous cities in Idumea, including Adora and Marisa.

(War 1:63)

Entrance hall to tomb in cave I at Marisa (biblical Mareshah), Hellenistic period. Carta, Jerusalem

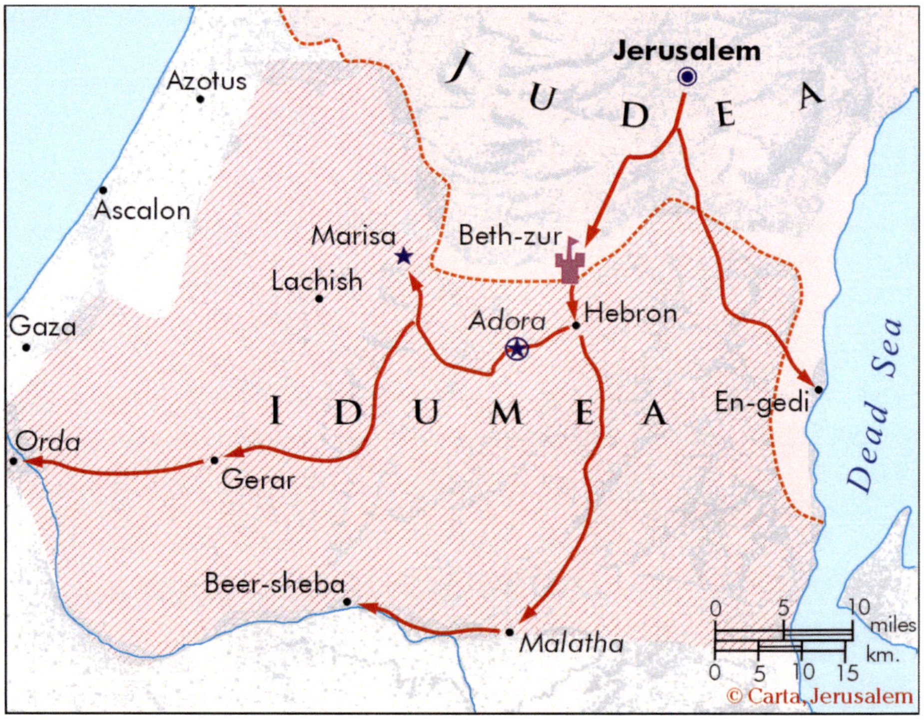

Judean border at succession of Hyrcanus

Judea

Hyrcanus' conquests

Maccabean fortress

Capital city

District capital

ANT. 13:257-258; WAR 1:63

Hellenistic onyx cameo (2nd century BCE) showing Antiochus VII. Kunsthistorisches Museum, Vienna. Author: Wolfgang Sauber (Via Wikimedia Commons)

Samaritans at Passover celebration at Mount Gerizim Source: Flickr Author: Flavio Grynszpan (Via Wikimedia Commons)

THE CONQUESTS OF HYRCANUS IN SAMARIA AND THE COASTAL PLAIN 126 TO 104 BCE

Before setting out against the Idumeans, Hyrcanus embarked on a campaign against the Samaritans. This people lived isolated in the mountains of Ephraim. Hyrcanus captured Shechem and destroyed the temple and the little town on Mount Gerizim. Their temple gone, the Samaritans henceforth focused their religion on an edition of the Pentateuch inscribed in an archaizing script like that used on Hasmonean coins. They did not join the mainstream of Judaism but continued (to this day) to preserve their unique identity.

Hyrcanus extended his domain in the coastal plain, too. Shortly after the death of Antiochus VII, he recaptured the districts temporarily lost in 132 BCE: Joppa, Gazara, Pegae, and "the harbors" (Apollonia and the port of Jamnia); before he died, he also held Jamnia and Azotus with its harbor.

After the annexation of Idumea and Samaria, Hyrcanus set out for his primary objective: the string of Greek cities that prevented Judea's expansion to the north and its union with Galilee. These were Strato's Tower, Samaria, and Scythopolis — forming a line from the sea to the river Jordan.

In 108-107 BCE, Hyrcanus began to beleaguer Samaria, whose inhabitants had provoked him and were further harassing the Jews of Marisa in the district of Nabrachta (mentioned in the Scroll of Fasting).

The siege of Samaria was protracted and difficult, the Greeks defending themselves valiantly. They appealed to Antiochus IX Cyzicenus for aid; he came to Scythopolis, but while proceeding to Samaria, a heavy defeat was inflicted upon him by Aristobulus I and Antigonus, the sons of Hyrcanus. The latter pursued him and captured Scythopolis (according to Josephus' Antiquities). In Josephus' War, however, they are reported to have purchased the city from the local commander, Epicrates.

At the same time the brothers had also invaded the Carmel area and possibly conquered the region of Narbata. Samaria was finally captured and partially destroyed by Hyrcanus (as evidenced in archaeological excavations) and its citizens exiled. The site, however, was resettled soon thereafter under Janneus. Thus, the way to Galilee was opened to the Jews.

On the twenty-fifth (day of Heshvan) the wall of Samaria was taken.
(Scroll of Fasting)

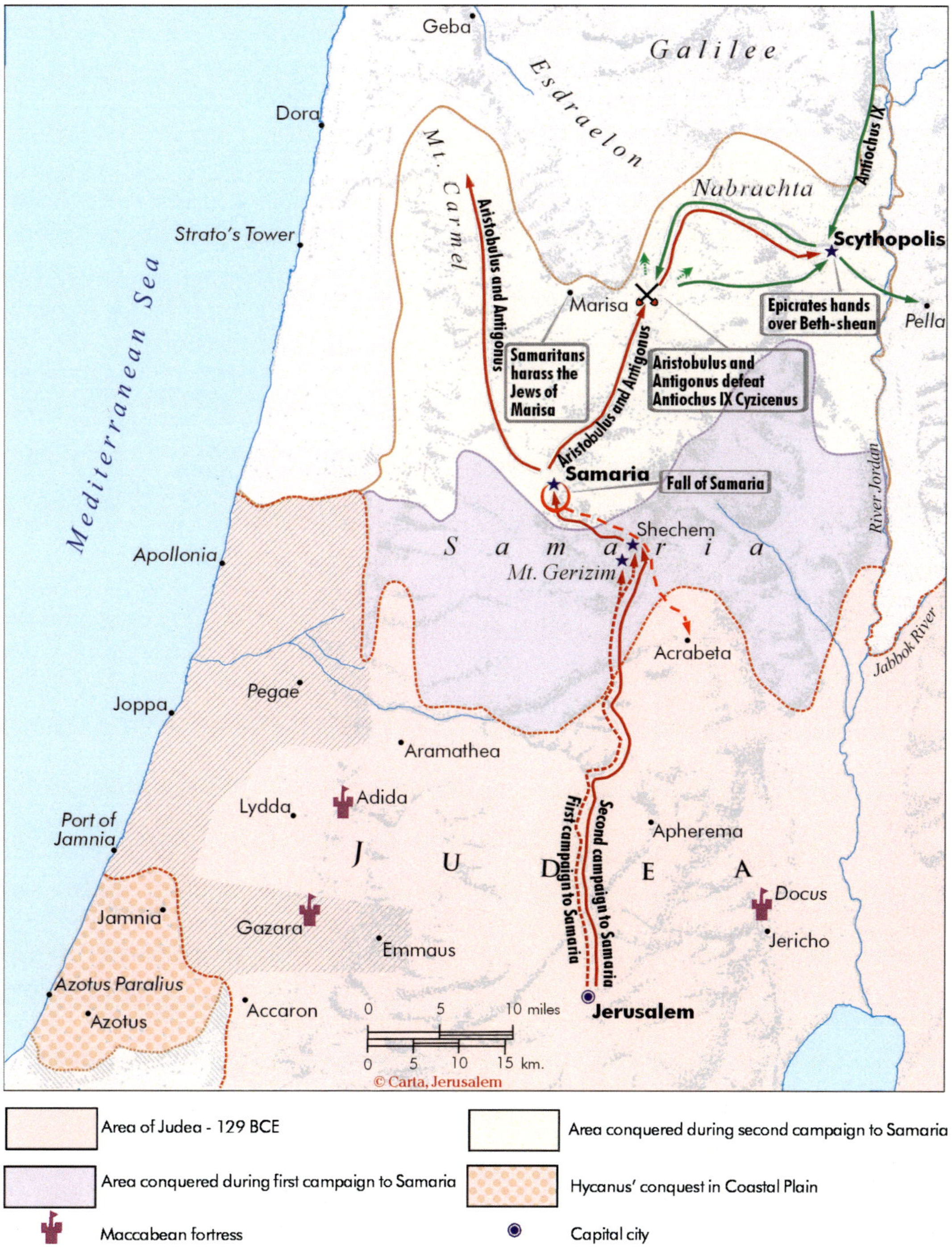

ANT. 13:255-256, 275-283; WAR 1:63-66; SCROLL OF FASTING, 21 KISLEV, 25 HESHVAN, 15-16 SIVAN

THE BOUNDARIES OF JUDEA ACCORDING TO THE BOOK OF JUDITH 108 TO 107 BCE

After this time every one returned to his own inheritance.

(Judith 16:21)

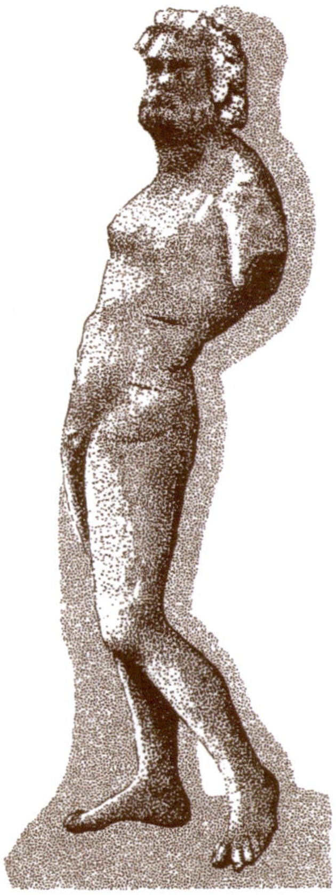

Statue of Hercules found at Samaria
Carta, Jerusalem

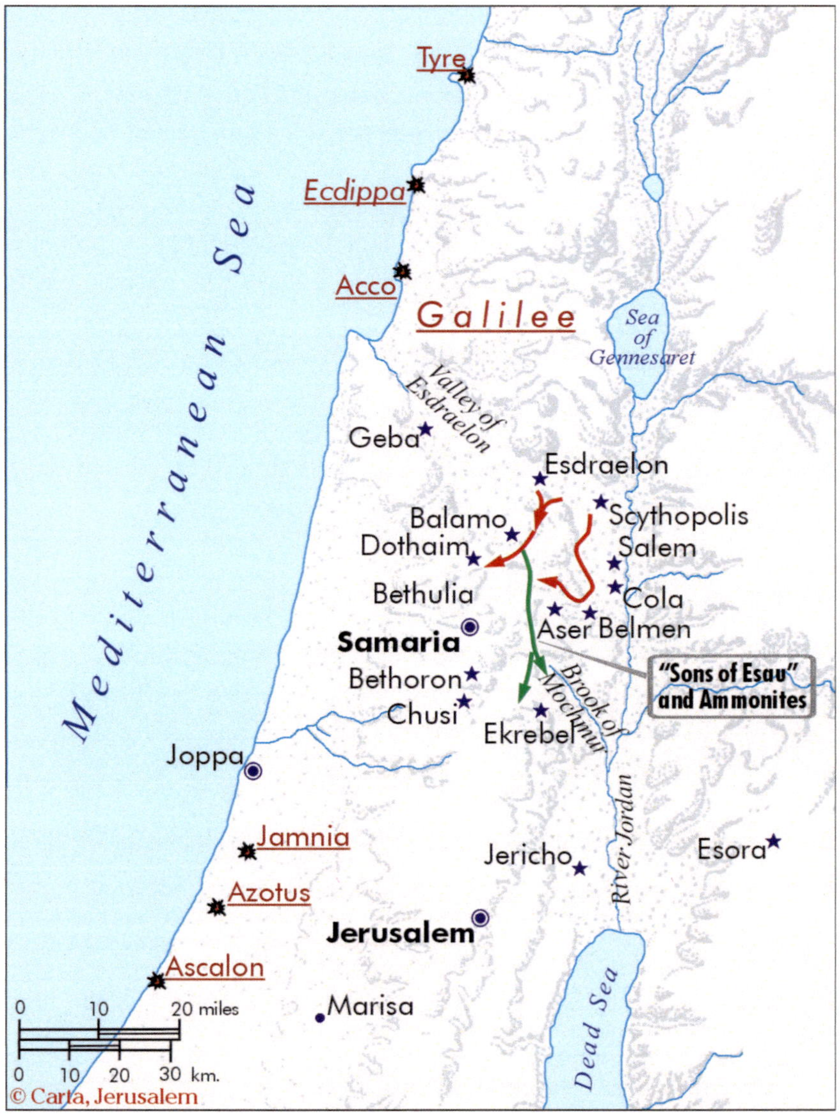

JUDITH 1:8-9; 2:28; 3:1-6, 10; 4:4, 6; 7:4

A story that is not historical in content often reflects the historical reality at the time of its writing. The Book of Judith seems to have been composed in the days of the siege of Samaria, although some scholars see it as an account of a war at the close of the Persian period. The Hebrew original is lost and only a Greek translation survives. This dating is based not only on the national-religious spirit permeating the book, but mainly on the boundaries of an imaginary "Israel" outlined by its author.

The Book of Judith, as a story, takes place in the days of "Nebuchadnezzar, king of Assyria" and relates of a town, "Bethulia" (similar to Beth-el, the "House of God," a synonym for Judea or Meithalun in northern Samaria), besieged by Holophernes, commander of the Assyrian army. Holophernes (a name appearing in the list of Persian satraps) was killed by the heroic Jewess Judith, after which his army dispersed in confusion. Both from what is included and from what is omitted in the story, we learn of the extent of Jewish rule within the historic reality of the period of the author. Thus, Nebuchadnezzar turns to the "nations of Carmel, Gilead and Upper Galilee" (Judith 1:8), and also to Sidon, Sur (Tyre), Ocina (Ptolemais), and Jemnaan (Jamnia), Azotus and Ascalon (2:28), indicating perhaps that these cities were not under Judean rule. Also, Holophernes encamped "against Esdraelon, near unto Dothaim. And he pitched between Geba and Scythopolis" (3:9-10), and from "Belmen [Abel-maim] ... unto Cyamon [Jokneam]." He sent troops of the "Sons of Esau" (Edomites) and Ammonites to Ekrebel (Acrabeta) which is near Chusi (Kuzi) on the brook Mochmur (Wadi Ahmar between Acrabeta and the Jericho valley; 7:18). To counter this danger, the "children of Israel that dwelt in Judea" sent messages to "the coasts of Samaria," Cola (Qa'un), "Bethoron [Beth-horon] and Belmen [Abel-maim] and Jericho and to Choba and Esora [Jazer] and to the Valley of Salem" (4:4). This serves to define a boundary of Judea, from Samaria to Jokneam and the Valley of Salem, south of Scythopolis, but excluding the latter itself, Geba, the Carmel, Jamnia, Azotus and Ascalon. The whole Jordan Valley and Transjordan up to Jazer were included. Ptolemais, Tyre, Sidon, Philadelphia, and Ascalon were independent cities.

ARISTOBULUS CONQUERS UPPER GALILEE
104 TO 103 BCE

This man was a kindly person and very serviceable to the Jews ...
(Strabo, quoted by Josephus, Antiquities 13:319)

John Hyrcanus lived to a ripe old age; when he died, he left a prosperous kingdom, in spite of the split between the rival Sadducees and Pharisees, a dissension that forebode evil days for Judea. His successor, Judas Aristobulus I, reigned for only one year, but in this short period he succeeded in conquering Upper Galilee. During his brief reign Aristobulus fought against the Itureans and, according to sources critical of the Hasmoneans, forced them to convert to Judaism.

The Itureans were a group of tribes of Arab origin which had banded together into a kingdom in the Beqa valley in Lebanon and on Mt. Hermon. The extent of their territory can be discerned from the pottery finds characteristic of these tribes. The Itureans apparently exploited the fall of the Seleucid empire and spread into the Upper Galilee and the Tiberias valley. (Lower Galilee was Jewish at this time.) Aristobulus took control of the Upper Galilee and raided the Iturean strongholds, but did not conquer their kingdom. The story of their forced conversion seems exaggerated like that of conversion of the Idumeans. Apparently Hasmonean policy was not that strident. It seems that social expedience over many decades eventually made the inhabitants of the Upper Galilee part of the Jewish people.

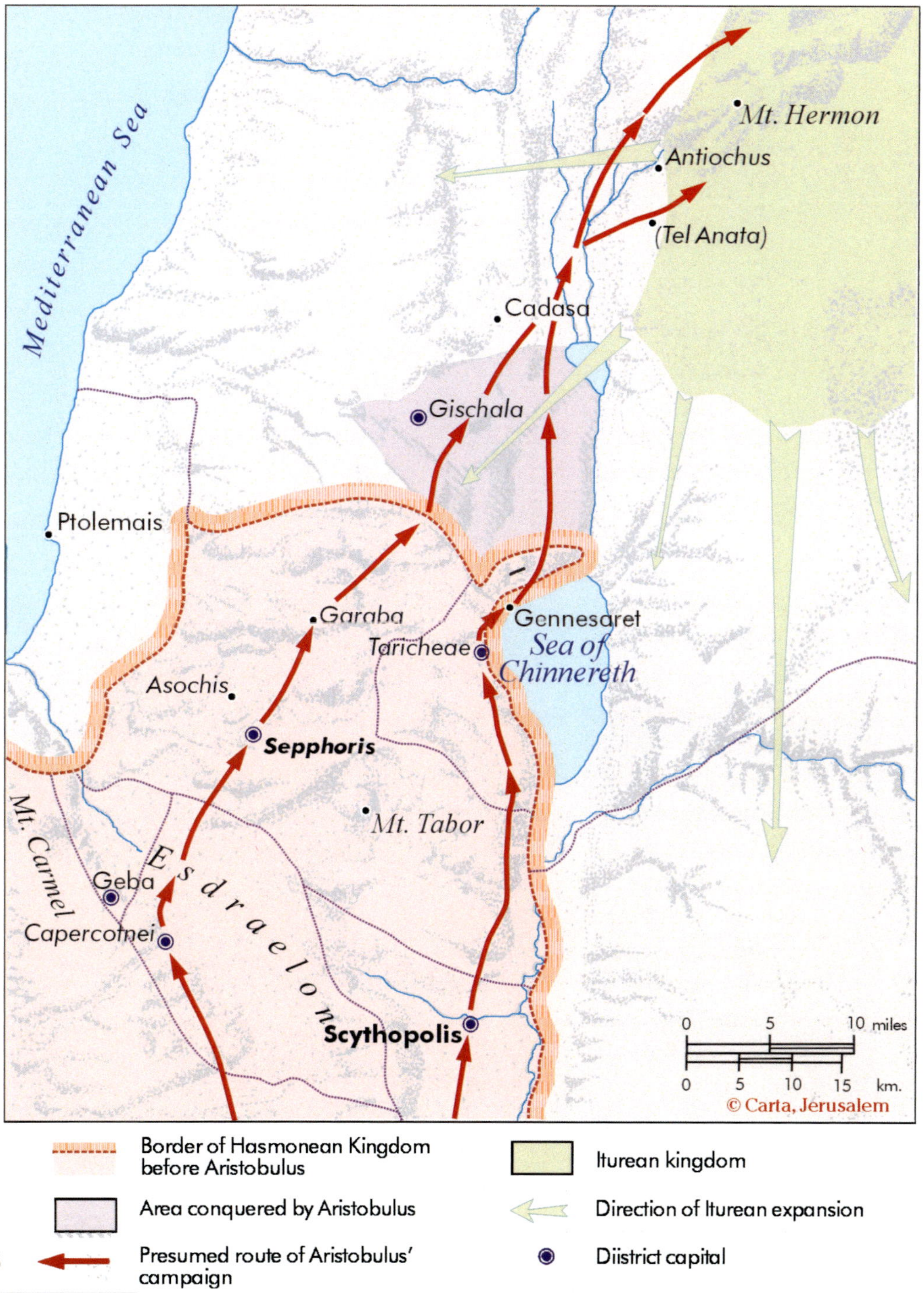

ANT. 13:319; WAR 1:76

Modern model of a Hasmonean warship, based on a sketch found in Jason's Tomb; National Maritime Museum, Israel
Author: Deror avi
(Via Wikimedia Commons)

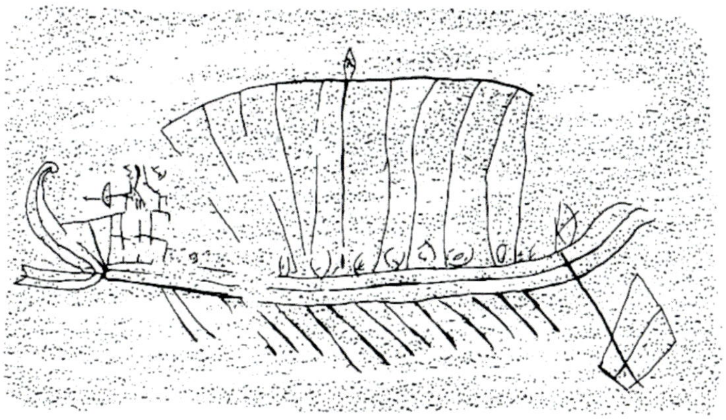

Warship sketch
(In Jason's Tomb, Jerusalem)
Carta, Jerusalem

THE KINGDOM OF ALEXANDER JANNEUS
103 TO 76 BCE

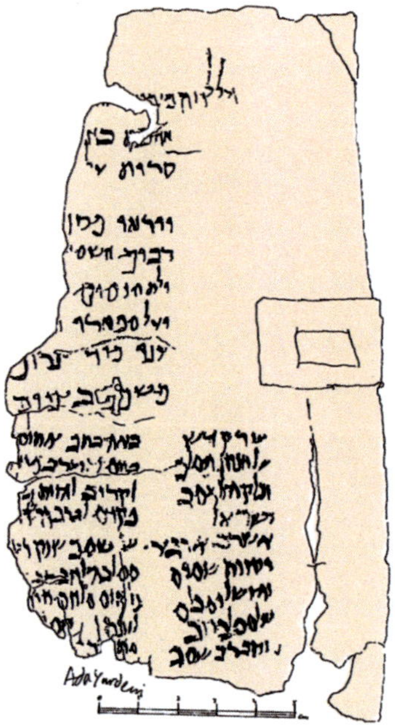

A song for the welfare of Jonathan the King (Alexander Janneus) Carta, Jerusalem

Coin of King Alexander Jannaeus: GNU Free Documentation License (Via Wikimedia Commons)

ANT. 13:395-404; WAR 1:106

Aristobulus' successor, his brother Alexander Janneus (103-76 BCE), completed the conquest of almost the whole of the Land of Israel. Although generally unlucky in the field, he succeeded through his perseverance in a series of campaigns, and added to the Maccabean domains Dora and Strato's Tower, together with the Carmel cape; Gaza and her satellite towns down to Rhinocorura on the Brook of Egypt; the lands surrounding the Dead Sea; and most of the lands east of the Jordan from Panias at the source of the river southward — only Philadelphia remained unconquered.

Alexander also succeeded in staving off various enemies — Ptolemy Lathyrus, king of Cyprus; the Seleucids Demetrius III and Antiochus XII; and the Nabatean kings.

He was less successful in the interior; dissension between the ruling dynasty and its Sadducee followers, and the Pharisees (who first rose under Hyrcanus) waxed under Janneus into a rebellion, subsequently suppressed with great cruelty.

Under Janneus, the Maccabean state reached its apogee.

POMPEY'S CAMPAIGN IN PALESTINE
63 BCE

After Janneus' death (76 BCE), his widow Alexandra reigned till 67 BCE. Upon her death, civil war broke out between her sons, Hyrcanus II and Aristobulus II. The former was weaker and, prompted by Antipater the Idumean (the evil genius of the Hasmonean dynasty), called Aretas, the Nabatean king, to his aid. The invaders besieged Jerusalem, but the Romans finally intervened.

Rome had gradually annexed the entire Hellenistic East after defeating the Seleucids. From 88 to 64 BCE she fought Mithradates king of Pontus, her most dangerous enemy in the East. In 64 BCE, Pompey, who finally defeated Mithradates, came to Damascus, annexed the Seleucid kingdom (which then became the province of Syria) and turned his attention toward Judea.

At first he sent Scaurus, one of his commanders, to Judea and ordered a truce. Aretas and Hyrcanus retreated (on their way back they were soundly defeated by Aristobulus at Papyron near the Jordan). Pompey next ordered the two rivals to appear before him; seeing that Hyrcanus was the weaker personality of the two, he chose him to rule over the Jews. Aristobulus retired to the fastness of Alexandrium, overlooking the Jordan Valley. Pompey followed him with his army, passing Dium (and probably also Gadara), Pella, and Scythopolis. At Coreae the Roman army entered Judea proper. Aristobulus negotiated from weakness and finally surrendered. Pompey then advanced to Jericho, where he learned that Aristobulus' adherents refused to surrender the capital; thereupon the Roman army — now in high spirits, for at Jericho news had arrived of the death of Mithradates of Pontus, Pompey's old foe — marched upon the Holy City.

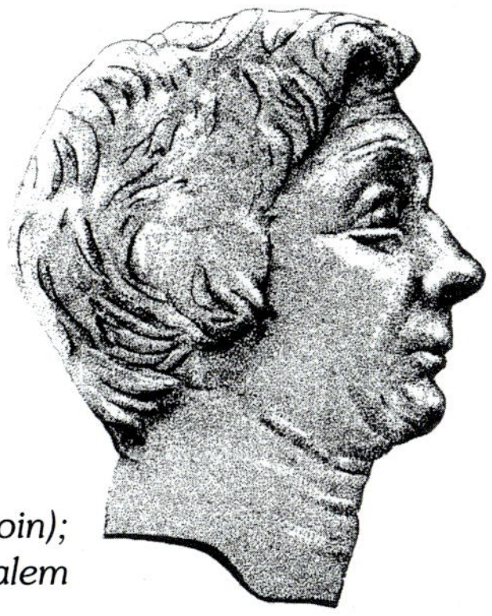

Pompey (Drawing from a coin); Carta, Jerusalem

Pompey ... took the army ..., and the auxiliaries ... as well as the Roman legions already at his disposal, and marched against Aristobulus.

(Antiquities 14:48)

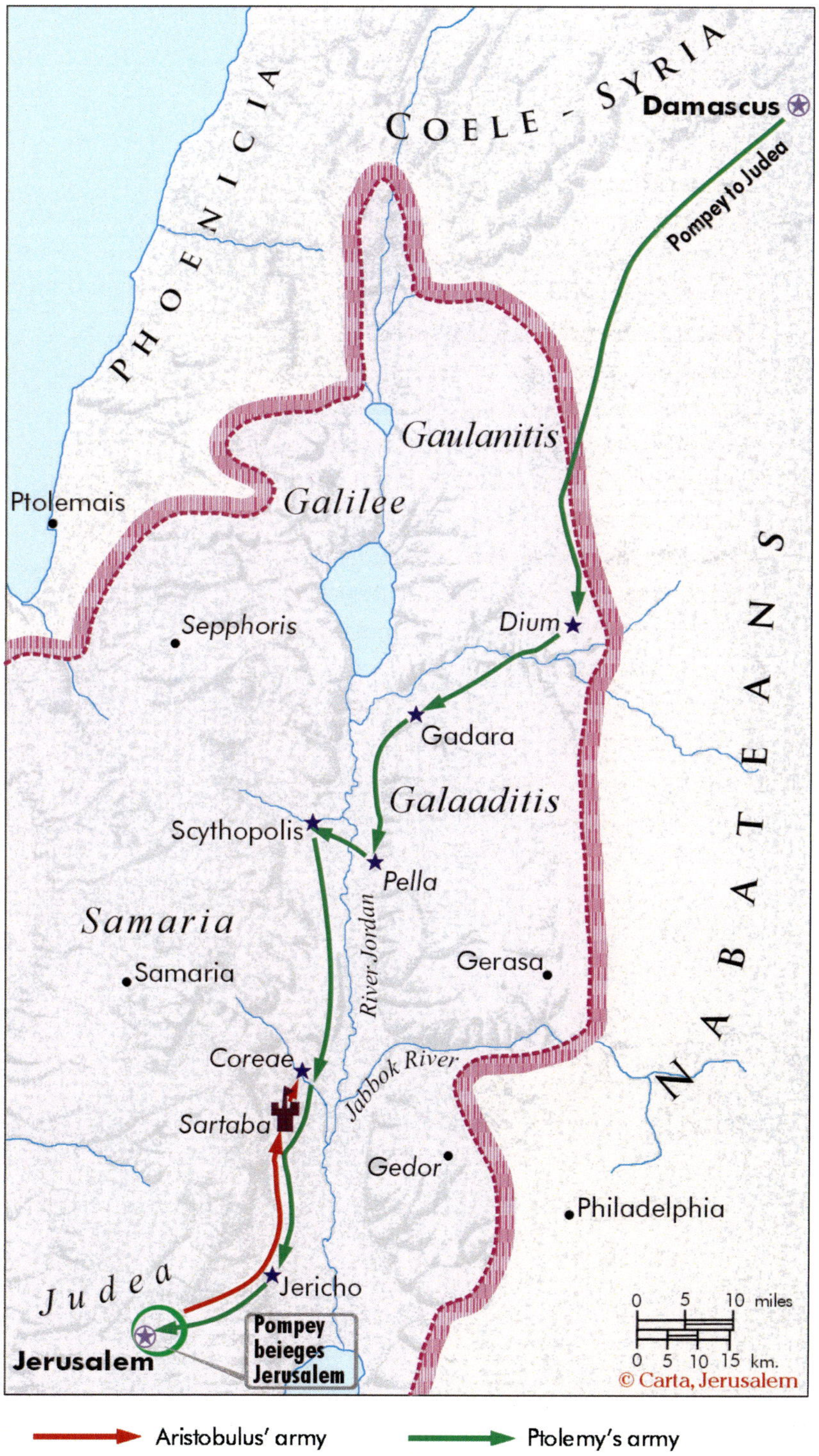

ANT. 14: 48-55; WAR 1:133-139

Petra, capital city of the Nabataeans
Author: Ameenalzubi
(Via Wikimedia Commons)

POMPEY'S SIEGE OF JERUSALEM 63 BCE

For we lost our freedom and became subject to the Romans, and the territory which we had gained by our arms ... we were compelled to give back ...
(Antiquities 14:77)

When the Roman army approached the gates of Jerusalem, it encamped to the south of the city. The Upper City and the king's palace were in the hands of Hyrcanus' partisans, who opened the gates to Pompey. Aristobulus' supporters demolished the bridge connecting the Upper City with the Temple and prepared their resistance from the Temple Mount and the nearby Baris. The Romans put a dike around the Temple fortifications and built a camp to the north. They prepared a two-pronged assault: across the fosse next to the "towers" of the Baris in the north and at the ruined bridge in the west. They built a ramp and positioned their siege engines and catapults. Work was facilitated by taking advantage of the Jews' reluctance to fight on the Sabbath: on this day, the Jews hesitated to interfere with the building of the ramps, unless physically attacked.

The assault finally came on the Sabbath, of course. The towers and the wall gave way, and the Romans invaded the Temple, but the priests continued the service as if nothing had happened. According to Josephus, twelve thousand people died on this one day. Pompey entered the Holy of Holies, but did not touch the Temple or its treasures.

ANT. 14:57-71; WAR 1:141-151

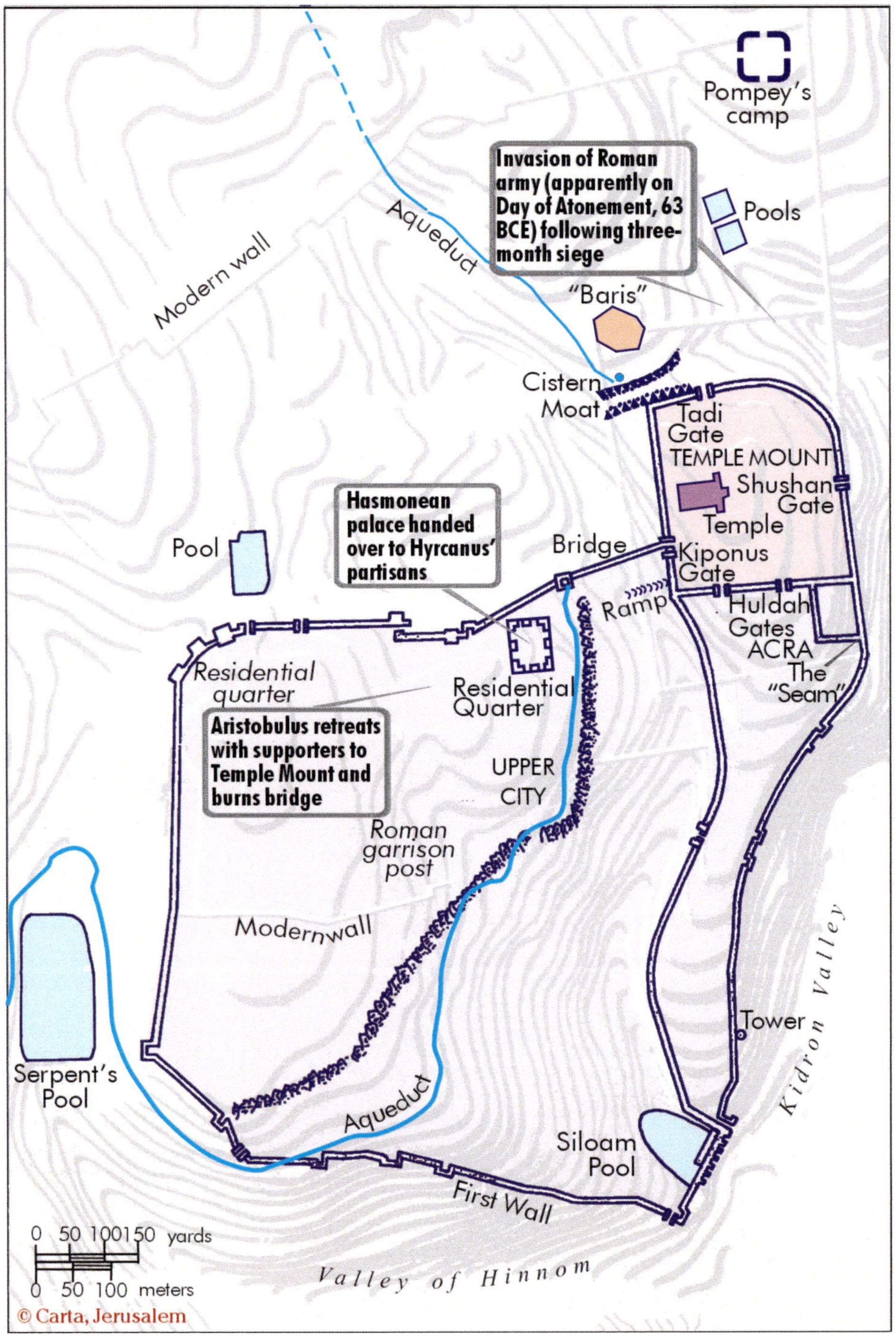

The Siege and Destruction of Jerusalem
Date: 1850
Source: Preterist ARTchive
Author: David Roberts (1796–1864)
(Reproduction of a lost oil painting.)
(Via Wikimedia Commons)

POMPEY'S TERRITORIAL ARRANGEMENTS 63 TO 55 BCE

The arrangements of Pompey after the conquest, completed by Gabinius (proconsul of Syria in 57-55 BCE) were relatively easy on the Nabateans, harder on the Itureans, and very harsh on the Jewish state. Pompey "liberated" the Greek and Hellenized cities occupied by the Jews since the days of Hyrcanus and subjugated their rural populations to these Greek cities. Thus, there again rose autonomous units (under the supervision of the Roman proconsul in Syria) such as: Gaza, Azotus, Jamnia, Joppa, Apollonia, Arethusa (Aphek), Strato's Tower, and Dora on the coast; in the interior: Marisa, Sebaste, and Scythopolis. Beyond the Jordan, Gadara, Hippus, Abila, Dium, Pella, and Gerasa were "reestablished." The Jews kept Judea proper, the eastern part of Idumea, Perea, and Galilee. The Samaritans became independent, and the plain of Esdraelon was detached from Galilee. Esbus was returned to the Nabateans who, except for being removed from Damascus, hardly suffered any diminution of the area under their control. The area of Lake Semechonitis, Panias, and Gaulanitis were given to the Itureans, but they lost their possessions on the Mediterranean coast.

The Carmel was returned to Ptolemais. The Jews held on to those areas that were densely populated by them, except Joppa and its neighborhood and the plain of Esdraelon. In all the Greek cities reestablished by Pompey and Gabinius, the populations exiled by the Maccabeans were returned. Hyrcanus II again became high priest in Jerusalem, but administration was entrusted to Antipater. Aristobulus II and his family were exiled to Rome.

During the rule of Gabinius, an attempt was made to split the Jewish State into five synedria (districts), a tactic applied by the Romans in Macedonia. The seats of the synedria were in Sepphoris (Galilee), Ammathus (Perea), Jericho, Jerusalem, and Adora (eastern Idumea). But the unity of the people could not be destroyed by such means, and the synedria were dissolved after a short time.

Judea profited from the civil war between Pompey and Julius Caesar. When Caesar emerged victorious, he pursued Pompey to Egypt and there became entangled in fighting at Alexandria.

In the ensuing events, Antipater was of great assistance to the relieving army of Mithradates of Pergamum and was duly rewarded by Caesar.

Hyrcanus II was appointed ethnarch by Caesar and Antipater as the effective administrator of the State. In appreciation of the help he had received from the Jews, Julius Caesar returned to them Joppa and the plain of Esdraelon. From then on Antipater was the actual ruler of the land. He appointed Phasael, his firstborn, as governor over Jerusalem and his younger son Herod, who was yet a boy, govenor of Galilee.

He also set up five councils and divided the nation into as many districts.

(Antiquities 14:91)

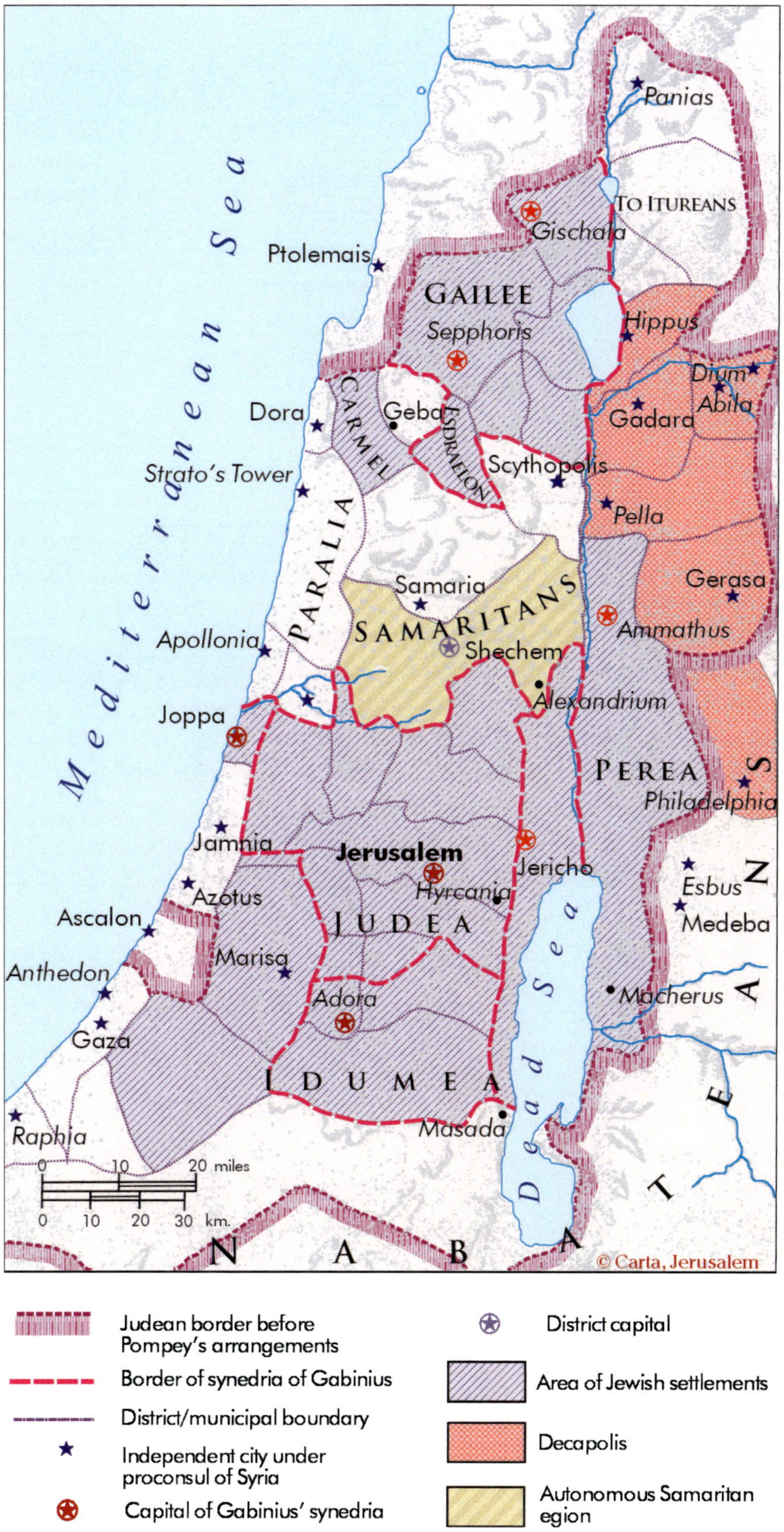

ANT. 14:74-76, 88; WAR 1:156-166, 169-170

The Hasmonean Family: Genealogy
165 – 4 BCE

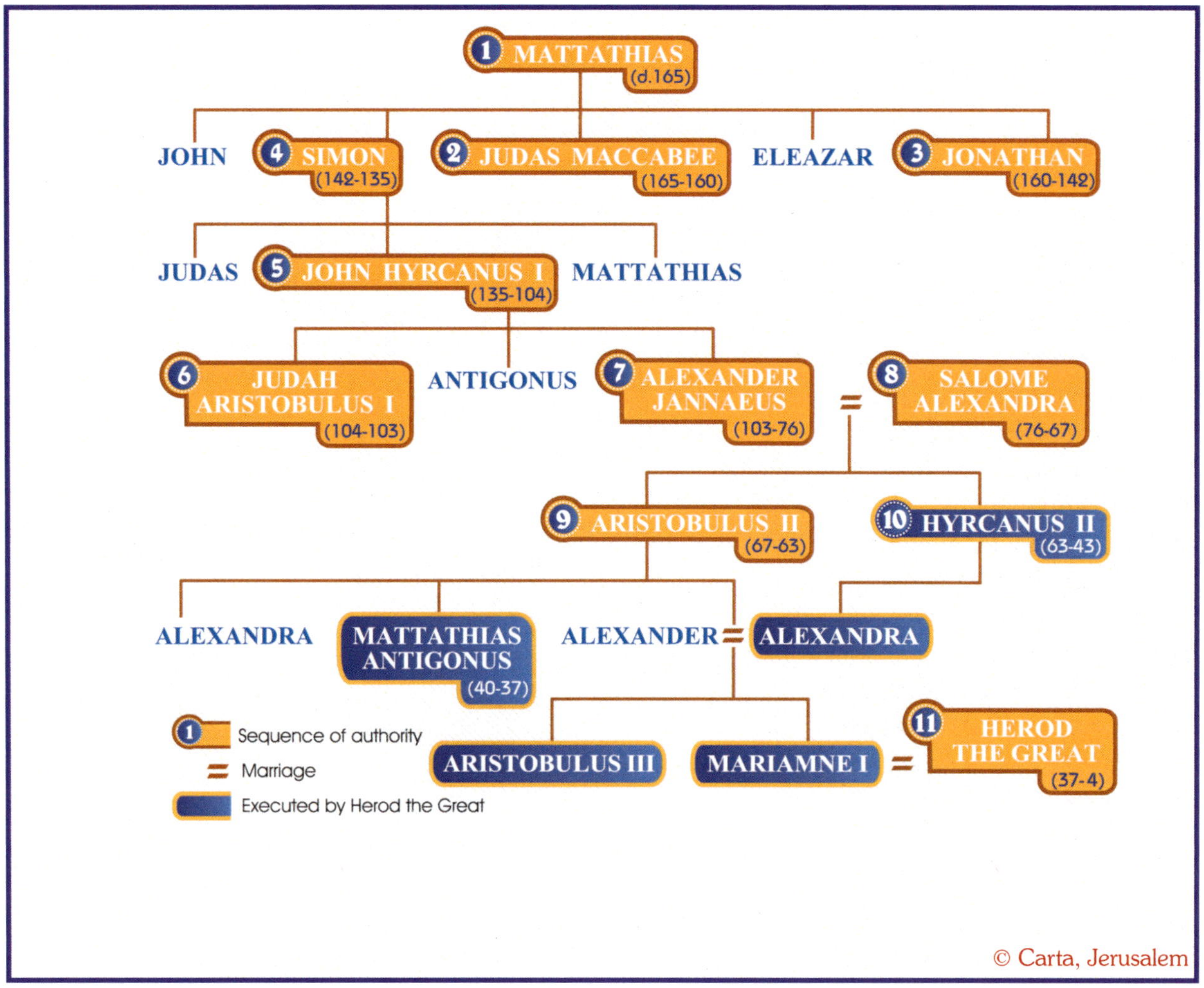

Index

C

D

E

G

H

I

J

K